LOOKING
BLACKWARD

OTHER BOOKS BY ARTHUR BLACK

Basic Black (1981)
Back to Black (1987)
That Old Black Magic (1989)
Arthur! Arthur! (1991)
Black by Popular Demand (1993)
Black in the Saddle Again (1996)
Black Tie and Tales (1999)
Flash Black (2002)
Black & White and Read All Over (2004)
Pitch Black (2005)
Black Gold (2006)
Black to the Grindstone (2007)
Planet Salt Spring (audio CD, 2009)
Black is the New Green (2009)
A Chip Off the Old Black (2010)

ARTHUR BLACK

LOOKING BLACKWARD

HARBOUR PUBLISHING

Harbour Publishing Co. Ltd.
P.O. Box 219, Madeira Park, BC, V0N 2H0
www.harbourpublishing.com

Cover credits: Author photograph by Howard Fry. Engraving, La Terre avant le déluge / Louis Figuier; ouvrage contenant 25 vues idéales de paysages de l'Ancien Monde, dessinées par Riou. 2nd Edition. Paris: Librairie de L. Hachette, 1863. Courtesy Biblioteca de la Facultad de Derecho y Ciencias del Trabajo Universidad de Sevilla.
Edited by Margaret Tessman
Cover design by Anna Comfort O'Keeffe
Text design by Mary White
Printed and bound in Canada

Canada Council   Conseil des Arts
for the Arts   du Canada

BRITISH COLUMBIA
ARTS COUNCIL
An agency of the Province of British Columbia

Harbour Publishing acknowledges financial support from the Government of Canada through the Canada Book Fund and the Canada Council for the Arts, and from the Province of British Columbia through the BC Arts Council and the Book Publishing Tax Credit.

Library and Archives Canada Cataloguing in Publication

Black, Arthur
    Looking blackward / Arthur Black.

ISBN 978-1-55017-590-5

    1. Canadian wit and humor (English). I. Title.

PS8553.L318L66 2012   C818'.5402   C2012-900326-33

To the Toronto Maple Leafs, from a guy who's old enough to remember the last time you won the Stanley Cup. Perhaps if somebody at head office knew how to spell the plural of "leaf" . . .

Contents

PART ONE

News from Planet Salt Spring

At Home in the Garden of Weedin'

*A garden is always a series of losses set against a few
triumphs, like life itself.*

—MAY SARTON

Newspapers.
     You'd think as an ink-stained veteran of the trenches of journalism I might have thought of newspapers as my gardening salvation, but no.

I've tried every other form of gardening—companion, raised bed, community, patio—even guerrilla gardening. (That's where, after you realize you're too late for planting and your garden plot has morphed into a writhing Congo of weeds with stems the size of Madonna's thighs, you stand on your balcony and empty your seed packets into the wind, go back inside, crank up the AC and watch reruns of *Seinfeld*.)

Newspaper gardening trumps all that. Last fall I diverted all those hernia-inducing bundles of newspapers I normally lug off to the recycling depot and spread them, section by section, on my garden plot. Come spring the dormant weeds that rule my garden try to punch through the soil to launch their customary takeover bid and lo! They are foiled by sun-blocking platelets of *Globe and Mail*, *National Post* and flyers from Home Hardware. (I envisage the weed seeds twisting their microscopic legume moustaches in frustration, muttering "Curses, foiled again!" then U-turning back into the soil to wither and die, har har!) The spring rains would turn the newspapers into pliable, nourishing mulch (publishers now use biodegradable inks). I would merely have to meander through my garden patch poking seeds hither and yon, like a tech-savvy Johnny Appleseed.

Mistake number one. Newspapers exposed to the elements turn into a lot of things over a Canadian winter—crusty yellowing scabs, airborne eyesores, cozy cave condos for mice, slugs and sundry creepy-crawlies—but mulch? Not so mulch.

Plus the spring winds arrived before the spring rains did. Most of my garden cover now lies in scattered clumps across my neighbour's backyard, although some got snarled in his trees and I'm pretty sure that's the sports section of the *Vancouver Sun* plastered against his chimney. I would make a point of sending over a bushel basket of harvest bounty—tomatoes, corn, carrots—to my neighbour as peace offering if, in fact, I could look forward to a bushel basket of harvest bounty.

I cannot.

It's only mid-summer but I can safely forecast that my autumn yield—tomatoes the size (and density) of ball bearings, ears of corn you could stick in your ear, and limp, wizened carrots that look like Hugh Hefner's worst nightmare—will not fill a bushel basket. A doggy bag maybe, but not a bushel basket.

People ask if I'm discouraged and I say no. Next spring I will once again arm myself with rake and shovel, trowel and watering can and transform myself into a true Son of the Soil.

Literally. It's a new approach I can't wait to try. I'm going to dig a hole in the centre of the garden about a foot and a half deep. Then I'm going to step into it, fill the dirt in around my boots, water and fertilize liberally.

Grow my own dope. It's a natural.

On Salt Spring, Fall is Fair

Ahh, autumn. Could the gods possibly offer up a finer season? "The berry's cheek is plumper," Emily Dickinson wrote. "The nuts are getting brown, the maple wears a gayer scarf, the field a scarlet gown."

All that and fall fairs too. Canada's dance card is speckled with autumn celebrations from the Trinity–Conception Fall Fair in Harbour Grace all the way across to the Sooke Fall Fair on the southwest tip of Vancouver Island. We love 'em. As entertainment, fall fairs are defiantly rural, endearingly innocent and just a touch hokey. *Jake and the Kid* country. They make you want to pop a straw hat on your head, stick a wheat stalk between your teeth, kick off your shoes and feel the dirt runnelling between your toes.

And I live just a pumpkin toss from one of the finest in the country.

The Salt Spring Island Fall Fair has roots that go back to 1896. Ever since—aside from a couple of world wars and a few fallow years in the middle of the last century—islanders have been coming together each September in a community do-si-do to celebrate summer's gentle demise and to mingle with the neighbours in full relaxation mode.

Our farm community isn't the defining force it once was, but plenty of folks around here still run horses or raise sheep and calves, chickens and ducks—and because it's Salt Spring, alpacas and llamas, emus and ostriches, too. You'll see them at the fair, along with the juiciest tomato, the tallest sunflower, the most flamboyant veggie/flower sculpture and the finest sheaf of wheat/oats/barley/rye/quinoa Salt Spring fields can offer up.

But it's about more than agriculture. Thanks to the almost embarrassing excess of musical talent on the island it's tough to get bored at the Salt Spring Fall Fair. When you want a break from the border collie trials or the sheep shearing competition, wander over to the open air stage (free admission, hay bale seating). If you time it right you'll catch Bill Henderson of Chilliwack fame in performance, or perhaps Valdy. Or Raffi—not to mention a host of less famous but equally talented acts. They are islanders all—and if Harry Manx or Randy Bachman isn't up on stage, look around. Chances are they're on the next hay bale, chowing down on a salmon burger.

The Salt Spring extravaganza nails all the usual fall fair familiars, along with a couple of offerings you won't find anywhere else—the Gumboot Dancers for instance. Thanks to the buckets of liquid sunshine we're blessed with, gumboots—the Brits call them wellies, you may know them as rubber boots, rain boots, barn boots or muck boots—are standard footwear on the Wet Coast for much of the calendar year. Gumboots are to Salt Spring as mukluks are to Pangnirtung and Manolo Blahniks are to Yorkville. A true Salt Springer is as comfy in gumboots as Karen Kain in ballet slippers or Sidney Crosby in a pair of Bauers. Just as graceful, too.

Well . . . nearly.

But a gumboot dance isn't a solo performance. It's a choreographed extravaganza involving up to a dozen performers and featuring much rhythmic calf-slapping and syncopated foot-stomping. Gumboot dancing is high energy, exceedingly merry and oddly beautiful. It is impossible not to grin idiotically when the Gumboot Dancers explode onto the stage.

And then there's the Zucchini 500. It operates under more or less the same rules that apply to the marginally more famous Indianapolis 500—there's an official track, designated pit stops, even "mechanics" on standby—but instead of race cars, you've got wheeled zucchinis. Anyone can enter (the younger the better), providing they show up with a modified zucchini under their arm. Just add a couple of axles and a set of miniature racing slicks (roller skate wheels are popular) and proceed to the elevated track. There, gravity and design innovation will determine who gets to stand in the winner's circle. Our most over-rated vegetable has never been more nobly employed.

There is a midway for the kids but it's the old-fashioned kind—bean bag tosses, ring-the-bottle, a fishpond with no water and "catches" for all. Kids love it. One year organizers rustled up a bunch of oversized cardboard boxes and cartons from island businesses, set them up in a chockablock maze and let the kids go crazy. Simple still works.

Speaking of simple, let me share my favourite moment from fifteen years of faithful attendance. The Salt Spring Fair takes place, fittingly, in the country, meaning a fair hike from what passes for bright lights here. The parking area fills up pretty quickly but you can catch a free shuttle bus from town. Last year as I was leaving the fair one of the buses waddled by ferrying a load of sated visitors back to town. All manner of sated visitors—locals and Maritimers, Prairie-ites and Oregonians, probably some visitors from Europe to boot. It was a warm evening, the bus windows were down.

And wafting out those windows, a spontaneous, if ever-so-slightly-off-key, vocal rendition of "You Are My Sunshine" in at least sixteen-part harmony.

Top that, CNE.

It's Beautiful. It's Arbutus

In 1895 they did a census on Salt Spring Island. They found settlers from Europe, Asia and the Sandwich Islands (read Hawaii)—even two Greeks, one Egyptian and a Patagonian. Four hundred and thirty souls in all.

Today, a century and a quarter later, the same island holds ten thousand residents and the demographic has broadened considerably, as befits a settlement in a multicultural nation like Canada. We now have homesteaders of Russian, Australian, Korean, even Calgarian extraction. And if by "Patagonian" those census takers meant "Argentinean," well, we've still got one of those too.

Make that ex-Argentinean. Antonio Alonso left Buenos Aires and eventually washed up on Salt Spring back in 1992. As Antonio recalls it: "I woke up one morning and I was here. There were mountains; there were rivers; there were many lakes and the ocean all around. There were eagles and herons and deer running everywhere. I saw the colours of the wildflowers, the rocks of Mount Maxwell and the magic of the forest. I laughed and laughed. 'Who brought me here?' I thought, 'What luck!' I promised never to go to sleep again."

True to his word, Antonio hasn't slept much since. His Argentinean-tinged English can be heard lilting through the stalls at the Salt Spring market and in the air over the soccer pitch when he indulges his other outside passion—playing for the Salt Spring Old Boys soccer team. He's fifty-seven, but still moves like a cat.

His first outdoor passion? Antonio's a sculptor. He turns and carves wood in a studio just outside his house. He's been crafting and selling his wooden works pretty much since he got here. He can work with any wood but his preference is arbutus—which probably doesn't mean much to any Canadian who hasn't been west of the Rockies. Arbutus is ornery as trees go. It prefers the Wet Coast and only rocky, inhospitable soil close to the ocean. It grows up crooked, on tilted trunks; looks like it's dying when it sheds its bark annually in great scrolling strips; drops leathery leaves that even the deer can't eat; and stays green all winter, even though it's a deciduous tree.

It's a hard wood and it burns well, but you need to buck it up and split it promptly after it comes down. Leave it too long and the wood "sets." After that it's like chopping concrete.

It's equally hard to work with. Arbutus splits and cracks. Polished wood bowls have been known to "morph" months after they're finished. What was once perfectly round begins to resemble an amoeba.

So why bother? Because arbutus wood is beautiful. It's full of imperfections—checks, splotches, burls and knots—but that's what defines its character. And arbutus has something else. When it's carved and sanded and polished by an expert—it glows.

Enter Antonio Alonso. He loves the arbutus imperfections. "I use them," he says with a smile. "I could choose to get rid of the cracks, but I love them."

A lot of other people love them too—especially when Antonio's finished with them. His bowls and platters and free-form burls have been coveted and bought up by customers throughout Canada as well as by customers from the US, Europe, Japan and Australia.

It's ironic. Salt Spring is a mongrel island, made up of people from all around the globe. And Antonio Alonso's Salt Spring creations now live on mantels and coffee tables in homes . . . all around the globe.

Now that's what I call Fair Trade.

Budolph the Red-nosed Buffalo

I'm not the first person to remark on it, but I'll say it anyway. Something happens to people when they move to Salt Spring Island. Even Mounties. I'm pretty sure that Staff Sergeant Danny Willis and his wife, Janice, were reasonably normal people when they moved here. That was five years ago. A lot can happen in five years and a lot did. Like Budolph, for instance. Salt Spring, like much of the province, is policed by the RCMP. We have six constables, one corporal and a sergeant.

Actually . . . seven constables if you include Community Constable Budolph. They all work out of the RCMP detachment, which is not hard to find. Just get on the main road and go 'til you see the buffalo. First driveway after that and you're there. The buffalo? That would be Budolph. Budolph the red-nosed buffalo. He stands outside the Mountie detachment night and day, his big head lowered toward the traffic zipping by. Budolph is pretty much life-sized and a bit of a cross dresser, if the truth be told. Last February around Valentine's Day he appeared decked out in cupid's wings, a bow and arrow and heart-shaped sunglasses. For St. Patrick's Day he showed up covered in shamrocks with a leprechaun hat perched between his horns. Come Easter he was wearing Bugs Bunny ears and had a basket of Easter eggs sitting between his front hooves.

And in June for graduation week Budolph showed up draped in a grad gown and a mortarboard hat with a bright red tassel dangling down his shaggy mug.

Budolph the red-nosed buffalo is the inspiration and creation of the aforementioned Janice Willis, wife of Staff Sergeant Danny Willis of the Salt Spring detachment. Nothing to it . . . really. She simply wired together some peony and tomato cages, stiffened them up some with a few aluminum tent poles, covered it all with bubble wrap and added some downspout eavestrough elbows for hooves. Then a kilometre or two of duct tape, a meticulously sewn fur coat, a bicycle tail light for the blinking red nose and voila. Community Constable Budolph, at your service.

You think a buffalo mascot is a Disneyesque stretch for Canadian Mounties? Think again. Mounties and bison go way back. Next time an officer leans through your car window listening to your explanation for doing fifty in a thirty, take a look at the Mountie crest. See that furry critter with the horns and the beard right in the centre of the crest? Dead ringer for Budolph.

And now the bad news: Budolph's creator, Janice Willis, is moving off the island. Her husband Danny's being transferred out. Happens all the time with the RCMP, but they're not going far—to Sooke, which is just down the road a piece, meaning they'll retain visiting rights. Which they'll need, because Budolph is not going anywhere. Hey, his fan base is here on Salt Spring. He's even got his own calendar on sale at stores all over the island. It tells his story and shows him in various get-ups and costumes. Proceeds from the calendar sales go to Salt Spring Eldercare and Meals on Wheels.

So we lose the staff sergeant and Janice, but at least we keep Budolph. Standing on guard, 24–7, in front of the Mountie detachment. Stolid. Indefatigable. Balefully surveying the passing cars.

And I like to think every once in a while a boozy driver weaves by, blinks and says to himself: "Did I just see . . . a buffalo . . . in a Mountie dress uniform???"

"That's it—I've had my last drink."

Crooks Not Ready for Prime Time

When it comes to crime on Salt Spring we ain't exactly Tijuana after dark. Or even East Hastings at high noon. Salt Spring has bicycle thefts, drunken beach parties and bozos who do donuts on the school soccer field and knock over mailboxes with baseball bats. We have underage drinkers and some shoplifting, kids driving without licences and some mom-and-pop grow ops back in the hills that are more threatened by deer and rabbits than black helicopters. But occasionally, just occasionally, we have criminal scenarios that would cause even a seasoned city crime reporter to shake his head.

Last week I'm coming out of a local supermarket and run into a Mountie quizzing one of the store clerks. "What's the problem?" I ask. (You can do that sort of thing on Salt Spring without getting tasered.) Cop explains that overnight "person or persons unknown" had stolen three large potted plants worth about $200 from the supermarket parking lot. I tsk-tsk and make my way to the Legion, about a three-minute walk, just the other side of the RCMP depot.

In the Legion parking lot I encounter another island Mountie taking down particulars from a Legion employee. "What's the problem?" I throw out again. This Mountie is more officious but he says over his shoulder that thieves tried to break into the Legion overnight. Choice of assault weapon: three potted plants. The heavy pots broke the windows effectively enough; they were less successful with the steel bars behind the glass. Hmm, a veritable Salt Spring crime wave.

I was about to inform the Mountie of the stunning coincidence of plants being stolen from the supermarket and plants being used as B and E tools at the Legion but he was busy barking orders and telling everyone not to touch anything. "We can dust those pots for prints," he explained. That's when another bystander reaches down into the long grass beside the parking lot and pulls out a grimy, heavily laden baseball cap.

"Think this might figure into the investigation?" asks the bystander. The baseball cap contains three bulging plastic baggies of what looks an awful lot like marijuana.

Picture the crime in progress as it must have unfolded. Three perpetrators—let's call them Larry, Curly and Moe—are driving around Salt Spring in the middle of the night developing a powerful thirst. They elect to assuage said thirst by: (a) stealing three heavy potted plants from a well-lit parking lot; (b) humping said plants right past the island's only police station to; (c) the Legion, where an unknown quantity of liquor awaits them.

But these are not mindless amateur brigands we're dealing with— no. Before they fill the air with flying flowerpots, one of them—perhaps it was Curly—or Larry—says, "Yo, Moe. Why dontcha take off yer hat and put our stash in it so it's safe?"

To summarize, our hardy band has risked hernias, police confrontation, jail time, lifetime criminal records and about $500 worth of grass in a gamble to win what might have turned out to be twenty-four cans of Lucky Lager.

I don't know where Canada's next batch of criminal masterminds will hail from but I'm willing to wager a potted aspidistra that you won't find the words Salt Spring Island on their driver's licences.

Assuming they still have their driver's licences.

From Broom to Bust

Hooray for the Scots. The world owes a bundle to those crusty Celts who scratched out a civilization on Great Britain's rocky forehead and then shared their gifts with the world. We can thank the Scots for . . . let's see. Well, there's porridge. And haggis. And bagpipes and argyle socks. We are in their debt for the ubiquity of plaid; for the heart-stopping intensity of curling; and for the trance-inducing fascination of Scottish country dancing.

But we in the Gulf Islands and BC Lower Mainland can thank the Scots for one other gift. We can thank specifically one Captain Walter Grant who in 1850 planted on his farm near Sooke a handful of precious seeds he'd painstakingly plucked in the Scottish highlands then carried across an ocean and a continent to his new home. Captain Grant it was who gave us the gift of broom.

Not the curling variety. *Cytisus scoparius.* Scotch broom. A tenacious Brillo pad of a plant that can grow to ten feet tall and thrive in anything softer than concrete. Each plant produces seeds by the tens of thousands that love to hitch rides on tire treads, animal hooves, hiking boot soles or simple wind or water. The seeds have the constitution of ball bearings. They can survive inhospitable conditions for up to eighty years and then spring to life. And inhospitable conditions barely exist for Scotch broom. The plant prefers lousy soil; it considers salt a condiment. It eats deserts for . . . dessert. Whereas nothing much eats broom because it's toxic. And nothing much else grows when it's around because broom chokes out everything else. It is the Australian rabbit of the plant world.

So why would anyone want Scotch broom in their life? Well, it's pretty, with its dark green leaves and bright yellow flowers. It's often the first sign of real colour in the spring and Lord knows it's not hard to grow.

What drives farmers around the bend is that Scotch broom is sold as an ornamental plant in nurseries. People take it home and plant it in their garden or backyard. Where, of course, it never stays.

What makes broom especially scary in the Gulf Islands is its high oil content. We have hot dry summers. And our roadways and transmission corridors, our clearcuts and erstwhile grasslands are all packed with a plant loaded with a highly flammable liquid. An army demolition expert couldn't ask for more.

All of which has brought us an evolving cultural event on the Gulf Islands. It happens semi-spontaneously several times a year usually in the spring and fall when islanders band together at specific sites and throw themselves a broom busting party. There's a special wrench you can buy, rent or borrow that will lever a broom plant right out of the ground. The plants are then gathered, dried and safely burned.

It's a rear guard action but it makes a noticeable difference—and like many group efforts it gives rise to a healthy sense of community involvement. Sometimes broombusters get to feeling so good they stop applying X-rated adjectives to Captain Walter Grant and the leafy curse he bestowed more than a century and a half ago. Like the bird lover who imported and released a few dozen European starlings into Central Park about the same time—he meant well.

And a community Broom Pull? Hey, it's not as exciting as a Highland fling or an aria by Susan Boyle, but on the plus side . . .

No bagpipes.

The Hundred-Mile Diet. Not

Know how you can tell spring has sprung on Salt Spring? Roadside farmstands. Rickety little wooden booths that look like miniature false fronts from an old Western movie. They stand at the end of many farm driveways representing capitalism at its finest. In spring they feature daffodils, fresh eggs. As the season warms they'll offer everything from A to Z: almonds to zucchini. All fresh, all hand-picked, direct from the farmer to you.

Not that you're likely to see the farmer. Our farmstands run on the honour system. Pick out what you like, leave the money in the box. Visitors to the island are amazed. "You mean you just take what you want and they trust you to pay for it???" Wouldn't work in New York or Toronto or even Vancouver, but it's been working here for years, decades, really.

Salt Spring was farm country long before it succumbed to B&Bs. Used to be the apple orchard of the West Coast. Salt Spring orchards supplied Vancouver, Victoria—even Seattle.

Then the Okanagan came on stream. With sophisticated irrigation systems, high-yield hybrid trees and fleets of refrigerated transport, the Okanagan was hi-tech. Salt Spring orchardists, with their beater pick-ups at the mercy of the whimsical ferry system, were strictly mom and pop. We still have great apples on Salt Spring but the best place to get them is at a roadside farmstand.

What the Okanagan didn't do to Salt Spring agriculture government regulations did. The island was once world-famous for its lamb—anyone who's tasted Salt Spring lamb knows why. In 2007 the government decreed that livestock had to be shipped off island for slaughter. More time, more expense and needless stress on the animals. Many Salt Spring farmers just gave up.

Our local supermarket had a special on lamb chops last week. New Zealand lamb chops. Talk about coals to Newcastle.

Same sad song for other commodities. Farmers can't sell their apple juice because it's not pasteurized in a government plant.

It's technically illegal to sell Salt Spring eggs because as delicious and healthful as they are we have no government inspector on island to officially bless them. Brian Brett, a Salt Spring farmer, poet and potter says, "In ten years time it will probably be illegal for us to grow vegetables for people." Alarmist? Maybe not. A recent survey shows there are 44 percent fewer cattle, sheep, pigs and goats than there were just five years ago and 54 percent fewer chickens, turkeys, ducks and geese.

Common sense tells us we should be cultivating local produce but lawmakers choke the soil with rules and regulations. Salt Spring has only half the livestock it had five years ago. How long before it disappears entirely—along with those charming, endangered roadside farmstands?

Oh well. It's not as if we'll starve. We'll always have California. And New Zealand. Won't we?

Kill the Bunnies? Oh Deer

There's an orchard across the road from my front gate. This morning when I went up to get the paper I counted the deer under the apple trees. Twenty-three. It's not a big orchard. My walk to the gate took me past my garden and the lettuce patch there. Well, what was supposed to be a lettuce patch. Rabbits. Lot more of them lately too. Don't think I'll bother with lettuce next year because our rabbits are multiplying like . . . well, you know.

Now Samuel Beddis, the fellow who laid out that orchard about a hundred years ago, wouldn't have seen those as two overpowering problems. He would have solved them swiftly and personally. Rabbit stew for lunch; venison for dinner. But Sam Beddis didn't have a Long Gun Registry to contend with—or any neighbours to complain about bullets and buckshot flying hither and yon. I don't know of any of my neighbours who own a gun and they couldn't use it here if they did. Where I live it is illegal—and thankfully so—to fire a gun close to human habitation.

But we do find ourselves with more wild deer and rabbits than we know what to do with. Reaction has been typically Salt Springian. One island resident has offered to open up her property to refugee bunnies.

Well, it's a cheaper solution than the one arrived at by the University of Victoria. They plan to airlift unwanted campus rabbits to a wildlife rehab farm in east Texas. I didn't make that up.

Nobody's come up with a solution for the surplus deer. Our Island Wildlife Centre simply ran out of room. They don't take orphan deer anymore. And increasing numbers of those deer, orphaned and otherwise (not the sharpest knives in the woodland drawer, these deer), wander onto our roads to be killed or crippled by cars and trucks.

So what's to be done—a cull? Hah. Nobody's going to start a public campaign to have SWAT teams of hunters going around capping rabbits and deer. Why? The Bambi/Bugs Bunny factor. They're too damned cute, that's why.

We are contrary critters, we humans, and we have a schizoid relationship with the other species that share our planet. Some we adore; others we eat. Some we let into our houses and up on our beds; others we consign to overcrowded feedlots, Auschwitzian battery farms and slaughterhouses. Curiously, we seem quite at peace with this bloody double standard.

Then we have the wild deer. We neither coddle them nor kill them; consequently they multiply like fruit flies. The town of Kimberley, BC, wants to put their deer herds on birth control. The mayor of Grand Forks has been on the blower to Victoria, begging for some action to shrink the estimated 350 deer now living within Grand Forks town limits.

Thing is, deer and rabbits have been living here for thousands of years without overpopulating the place. But we also had cougars and wolves and bears for most of those thousands of years.

Cougars, wolves and bears didn't fit into our agricultural plans on Salt Spring so we shot them down and trapped them out. Now, aside from a few feral housecats and the odd faster than average eagle, fawns and rabbits have little to worry about on this island. Except perhaps starvation and disease.

Our local politicians claim their hands are tied. Our MLA says it comes under federal jurisdiction. The feds? They haven't got back to us.

Some mornings when I walk out to get the paper and count the deer, I hear this weird cackling sound overhead. I can't figure out if its wind in the poplars, or a skein of geese flying over . . .

Or the ghost of old Sam Beddis laughing up his shirt sleeve.

That's Ms. Monolith to You

Five thousand years ago, give or take a few centuries, some people gathered together on a stony plain about a hundred miles west of what would one day be the city of London and decided that this would be a good place to do it. The "it" was Stonehenge, a mysterious gaggle of massive stones half buried in the earth, arranged in patterns that experts with computers and X-ray scanners are still trying to unravel. Some of the stones weigh twenty-five tons; some came from 240 miles away. Construction and modifications, an estimated thirty million man-hours worth, occurred over a period of fifteen centuries. This by primitive people without an engine, a wheel or a written language.

Construction stopped on Stonehenge about the time the Crusaders were laying siege to the city of Acre in Galilee, but it has never stopped fascinating people in the thousand years since. Tour buses still roll up daily. Parts of the site have to be cordoned off to prevent the wear and tear of too many hands and feet. And here's the thing about Stonehenge: we don't really know what it's about. Oh, there are theories. It's an astrological observatory, a Druid shrine, a burial catacomb, a marriage centre, an extra-terrestrial teleportation site, an all-purpose, one-stop religious mall or all of the above. But no one really knows. The greatest thing about Stonehenge is its abiding mystery.

Which brings us, circuitously enough, to Salt Spring Island, where on an afternoon in the early years of the current millennium a group of people stood on a treeless hill overlooking Ganges Harbour and decided this would be the place to do it. The "it" in this case being to raise a

Stonehenge-like structure—not as massive, but pretty massive; not as labour intensive but a lot of hard work all the same.

The result is the Standing Babas—thirteen tall and irregular sandstone rocks, some of them towering sixteen feet in the air, half buried in the earth, along with eight additional smaller rock sculptures. The work is a collaboration. John LeFebvre who owns the land had the idea, Ron Crawford, a well-known sculptor, worked out the design with LeFebvre and stonemason Terry Biemen.

They had help that Bronze Age Stonehengers couldn't call on—cranes, front-end loaders, hydraulic saws, dump trucks—which is why they could complete their work in eighteen months instead of fifteen centuries. The result is definitely arresting. They call it Standing Babas in reference to the Khareshwari, Hindu mystics who take a vow not to sit or lie down for twelve years.

How long will Salt Spring's Standing Babas stand? Surely more than twelve years, but probably not forever. They're made of sandstone after all, which erodes over time. But they are sunk in the earth and they rest on reinforced cement pads and Crawford, their creator, reckons they're probably good for oh, the next fifteen hundred years or so. That's a pretty good poke. Fifteen hundred years ago the Mayans were in charge in Mexico and the Vandals were sacking Rome.

And Salt Spring fifteen hundred years from now? Safe to say it would be unrecognizable to us, no matter what goes down in terms of geological activity or human folly in the interim. Unrecognizable except perhaps—just perhaps—for that strange configuration of twenty-one giant stones standing on a hill overlooking the ocean.

Who knows what mythologies our descendants will weave around those?

All the News That's Fit to Drift

For me, one of the finest (because it was comprehensible) things Marshall McLuhan ever said was about newspapers. "You don't read a newspaper," said McLuhan. "You get into it . . . like a warm bath."

Folks on my island are lucky. We get our warm bath once a week— Wednesday afternoon, weather permitting. It's called the *Gulf Islands Driftwood*. Started off as a blurry, five-page mimeographed handout fifty years ago. Last week's edition ran to ninety-two pages.

Imagine that—half a century of reportage on floods, forest fires, felonies and miscellaneous tomfoolery that constitute life on the southern Gulf Islands. How does a paper stay successful that long? Partly by being pretty darned good. I write for about fifty weeklies across the country and it isn't homer patriotism that makes me say the *Driftwood* is the best of the lot. Week in, week out—it really is.

And I'm not the only one that thinks so. Every March the Canadian Community Newspapers Association announces the names of the best newspapers in the country. This year's winner in its circulation category right across Canada: *Gulf Islands Driftwood*. Just like last year. And the year before that.

The *Driftwood* has something sprinkled into its weekly recipe that most papers lack—a sense of humour. Every week, for example, the editors publish a "Rants and Roses" section in which readers get to cheer or jeer the island institution of their choice. The roses are pretty treacly stuff but the rants? Woo-hoo. Sulphurous, vituperative and blunt. Put it this way: you leave your garbage by the side of the road on Salt

Spring and chances are you'll be seeing a description of yourself in the *Driftwood* that you wouldn't want your mother to read.

And then there was the time the *Driftwood* almost caused a riot. The paper came out with a front-page photo of a sign posted on a vacant lot in downtown Ganges. "SITE OF THE NEW MCDONALD'S," the sign read.

McDonald's restaurants go with Salt Spring like Don Cherry goes with a Swedish underground film festival. That mind-blowing edition of the paper came out just about the time of year you'd expect. April . . . first, to be exact. Gotcha, Salt Spring. I wouldn't be surprised if Derrick Lundy* wasn't behind that photo stunt. He's been the chief photographer at the *Driftwood* for the past twenty-one years and the sight of Derrick flying by in his jeep with a couple of Nikons slung around his neck is as familiar as that row of pigeons on the roof of Mouat's hardware store.

Reminds me of the big forest fire we had a few years back. Derrick, rushing out to cover the blaze, thinks: "Aerial photos." Well sure. Go down to the harbour and get a seaplane to take him up right over the blaze. Derrick makes a call to Salt Spring Air, buckets down to the Ganges dock in his jeep. There's a seaplane waiting, pilot at the wheel, props spinning. Derrick, cradling his camera with the telephoto lens, jumps in. "Go, go, go!" he yells. The pilot takes off, a bit bumpy, but still they're airborne. But then Derrick notices they're flying away from the fire. Derrick yells to the pilot to turn back the other way.

"Why?" says the pilot.

"Because I'm a newspaper photographer," says Derrick. "I'm here to get photos of the fire."

"Oh," says the pilot. "So you're not the flying instructor?"

I'm not entirely sure that story would get past the *Driftwood* fact checkers, but if it isn't true, it oughtta be.

---

* Salt Spring Island abounds in anomalies; one of the minor ones is the D. Lundy conundrum. The island really does have two D. Lundys and their first names both sound like that frame work you see over oil wells. The difference is spelling. Derrick Lundy is the award-winning newspaper photographer and stonemason who looks like a Greek god. Derek Lundy (see the following page) is the award-winning author and world-class sailor who looks like Sir Francis Drake. Some day I plan to write about the hilarious misunderstandings that have arisen from this homonymical unlikelihood, but I have to wait until at least one of them dies.

A Borderline Case

You just never know about BC people, do you? Take the guy I shoot pool with every week. Name's Derek Lundy. He's in his early sixites, tall, lean, full head of grey hair, neat trim beard. Bit of an Irish lilt, somewhat Britified by a childhood in England and all but obliterated by the finishing school of southwestern Ontario. If you met Derek Lundy, now of Salt Spring, you would find him charming, politely inquisitive, knowledgeable, well spoken . . .

It would never occur to you that the man is crazy. Occasionally, I mean. Most of the time he lives a relentlessly normal life here on the island. Plays viola, sits on the library board, attends poetry readings and classical music events. But every few years or so he puts down his viola bow or his pool cue and does something utterly insane. And then he writes a book about it.

A few years ago he decided to visit Northern Ireland, where he hadn't lived since he was a child, and write about the Troubles—the sectarian violence that has plagued that fractious isle off and on since, well, forever.

This was no light undertaking. In parts of Northern Ireland the name Lundy carries the cachet of Benedict Arnold or Vidkun Quisling. That's because a certain Colonel Robert Lundy is considered to have sold out to enemy forces. Happened a little over three centuries ago but the Irish, particular Ulstermen, have long memories. And here's Derek waltzing into Londonderry taverns and meeting halls and chirping: "I wonder if I could chat with you about the Troubles. The name's Lundy . . . "

Mr. Lundy survived. And the result was a best-selling book called *The Bloody Red Hand*.

Before that, sailing caught his fancy. He decided to write about that. By way of research he crossed the Atlantic in a square-rigger and also made it around the much-dreaded Cape Horn—under sail.

The result: two bestsellers—*The Way of a Ship* and *The Godforsaken Sea*.

And then Lundy decided it might be nice to go for a motorcycle ride. No matter that he hadn't sat on a motorcycle for twenty-five years. He bought a shiny red Kawasaki 650 and rode the Mexican–American border. All of it. From the Gulf of Mexico to Tijuana on the other side of the continent. When he was done he shipped the bike north and rode the Canadian–American border. All of it. From Calais in Maine to Neah Bay, Washington.

He survived. Ten thousand kilometres of mountains and turnpike, forest and desert, bad roads and worse people. Banditos. Drug runners. Redneck vigilantes. Unsmiling border guards behind mirror sunglasses who greet you with a hand on their gun and a snarl on their lips. He survived that too—and got a book out of it called *Borderlands: Riding the Edge of America*.

It's not a fun read but it's a fascinating one—about something that affects all of us here in BC, living above that thin pink line running from Glacier National Park all the way to the Strait of Juan de Fuca.

It is no longer part of that great, undefended border "guarded only by neighbourly respect and honourable obligations" that Winston Churchill so admired. From gunboats on the Great Lakes to surveillance drones over the Rockies, post-9–11 paranoia has turned a largely invisible line into a bristling fortification. Lundy's book *Borderlands* catches the border in transition and he warns us that the Canadian tradition of "popping over the border" is gone, almost certainly forever. Robert Frost once said, "Good fences make good neighbours." I'm not sure this is the kind of fence he had in mind.

As for what's next for Derek Lundy, I wouldn't hazard a guess. My advice: If you see a grey-haired guy bearing down on you crouched on the back of a dusty red Kawasaki 650—dive for the ditch.

Man's crazy.

My Garden Needs a Guardian

I am not the world's greatest gardener.

I try. Every spring I purchase precious packets of organic seeds at prices that would make a Yonge Street smack dealer blanch. I consecrate my plot with lashings of fertilizers, soil conditioners, weed deterrents and germination enhancers. I subdivide it into serried rows behind cute wee signs that read LETTUCE, CARROTS, TOMATOES and BEANS. Then I sow, hoe, mulch and pray religiously according to the dictates of the Holy *Farmer's Almanac*—and I wait.

And if I listen very carefully I can hear (just over the munchings of potato beetles, cabbage maggots, corn borers, cutworms, earwigs and banana slugs) the Gardening Gods snickering up their celestial sleeves. My annual crop is a cruel and twisted parody of agriculture. What were promised to become beefsteak tomatoes emerge, grudgingly, as tiny marbles, hard as jade and just as tasty. My Yukon Gold potatoes look like malignant tumours. My lettuce is listless, my peppers pathetic, my beets are beat and my carrots are DOA.

Each year I discover new ways to fail at gardening and I'm not getting any younger. I confess I was ready to turn in my Lee Valley polyurethane knee protectors and take up a less demanding pastime—sword swallowing or running with the bulls, perhaps.

But then I discovered *Heracleum mantegazzianum*.

Actually it discovered me. It appeared in my garden as if by magic, a vegetative colossus every bit as magnificent as its moniker. The single plant towered over my puny vegetables—a good fifteen feet high—with leaves like elephant ears, crowned with a majestic canopy of white flower clusters as broad as a beach umbrella. You're familiar with Queen Anne's lace, that common weed of ditches and vacant fields?

Think Queen Anne's lace—on steroids.

What a beauty. I intended to get a picture of my Sweetie standing under it, her arms encircling the three-inch diameter stalk, but I never got around to digging the camera out.

Just as well—she'd probably still be swathed in bandages, if not walking with a white cane.

Turns out that *Heracleum mantegazzianum,* better known as giant hogweed, is a monster worthy of Stephen King. Tiny hairs on the stem and leaves contain a toxic sap that sears human flesh, produces painful, oozing blisters and ugly scars that can last for years. The sap also causes phytophotodermatitis, a condition that renders the victim allergic to the sun. And if it gets in your eyes it can blind you.

How did it end up in my garden? A fatalist might suspect malicious divine intervention. More likely the agent was an incontinent starling passing overhead.

The bad news: giant hogweed is showing up uninvited in gardens, riverbanks, bogs and vacant lots from Newfoundland to Vancouver Island. The good news is it's relatively easy to spot—especially when full grown. The telltale signs (aside from being as lofty as Steve Nash standing on Le Bron James' shoulders): a hollow stalk spotted with reddish-purple blotches and stiff hairs. DO NOT TOUCH. At least, not with bare hands. Me? I put on Tyvek coveralls, a balaclava, safety goggles and rubberized gloves to take my giant hogweed down. Then I chopped it up, double-Hefty-bagged the remnants and tried to figure out what to do next. Bury it? Dumb idea. Burn it in the backyard? I don't think so. A mature plant contains up to 50,000 hardy seeds that remain hot to trot for up to ten years. Experts advise putting it into a landfill site, but that makes me nervous too.

It occurs to me that what I need here is magical, not divine, intervention. I'm sending my toxic bundle off to the pros who run the only School of Witchcraft and Wizardry I know.

Hogwarts, naturally.

Rodney: Pure and Simple

Well, the winter winds have come and gone and they took a lot of Salt Spring trees with them. This winter also toppled one piece of island timber I never expected to see fall: Rodney Filtness. Rodney Frederick Charles Filtness, to be precise—but just plain Rod or Rodney to his innumerable friends and admirers. Born in Cuckfield, England back in 1949, Rodney migrated to where he belonged early on and spent most of his adult life here on the island. He was part of the warp and weave of the place. Ran at least three different restaurants at different times, all of them legendary; was an ever-smiling fixture at an early commune back in the sixties that is still remembered for its nude volleyball games.

Must have been something to see.

Rodney was a big guy. A very big guy. He was probably about a hundred pounds past the upper limit of the guidelines for Adult Body Weight classification laid down by Health Canada but Rodney's girth was pretty much irrelevant. Like Santa's. Or the Buddha.

Besides, he didn't move like a heavy man. More like a cat burglar. He was light on his feet and a superb dancer. And, in the winter months when he went to Mexico, a tireless body surfer who moved through the combers like a great sleek orca.

Garrison Keillor said, "They say such nice things about people at their funerals, it makes me sad that I'm going to miss mine by just a few days."

I think Rodney would have liked the service he got. Simple and quiet. A minimum of ceremony, a few heartfelt songs from friends. And remembrances. One young girl remembered sitting a table in one of his restaurants up to her ears in a volume of *Gray's Anatomy*. "What are you studying?" Rodney asked. "Anatomy," she told him. Rodney laughed. "Get yourself a boyfriend," he advised.

"Funny," the girl recalled, "how Rodney always said just the right thing."

Indeed. Another woman recalled a bad time in her life when she buzzed into a coffee shop, harried, distracted, depressed. Rodney appeared like a rosy planet, enveloped her in a hug and murmured in her ear, "How are you, my dear and precious one?"

"Those were exactly," said the woman, "the words I needed to hear."

We have a small, secluded pothole swimming lake on the island that is . . . well, not so much "clothing optional." You'd actually look a little goofy if you showed up there in a bathing suit. One woman at Rodney's memorial told of the summer evening she showed up at the lake, hoping to enjoy a sundown swim by herself. But finding Rodney treading water, naked, by the dock.

"He piggybacked me all around the lake," she said. "We laughed and sang and laughed and sang."

That would be Rodney, alright. A big man, but light.

Pure light.

PART TWO

Take Off, Eh?

Still Car City after All These Years

Detroit, Detroit
Got a helluva hockey team

—Paul Simon

If you travel far enough in this herky-jerky world of ours, sooner or later you will find yourself in one of humanity's less successful experiments in socialization. It may be an African shantytown or a Brazilian *favela*, a *banlieue* of Paris or a Manchester slum. But chances are it'll be closer to home—Vancouver's Downtown Eastside, say, or a roachy, dead-end street in Toronto's Parkdale district. Wherever it turns out to be you'll know the rules have changed because your long-dormant primordial instincts will kick in. Adrenalin will begin to prickle your gut. You'll feel more alert, slightly unsafe. The hairs on the back of your neck may begin to stir.

I know all about this sort of thing. I recently flew into Detroit.

"Brace yourself," I told my flying companion. "We're about to enter the Third World."

It's not like I was announcing breaking news—everybody knows Detroit's on the skids. In the past decade it's lost 25 percent of its population. One-third of Detroit's 140 square miles is derelict. YouTube is speckled with videos that show rotting factories, gutted ballrooms and deserted office buildings.

The industrial juggernaut that once manufactured four out of every five automobiles in the world is a skeleton of its former self. Ford and GM alone have axed 70,000 jobs in the past few years. Corrupt politicians, collapsing public schools—I knew we were headed into an urban no-man's land once our plane taxied up to the gate. I just wanted to be sure my travelling companion wasn't too shocked when we deplaned.

We were shocked. By the airport, for starters. It moves thirty million passengers a year, making it one of the busiest on the continent. Detroit is a transportation hub for all North American airlines and the Asian gateway for Delta, the largest airline in the world. What's more the airport is not dingy like Pearson, bewildering like La Guardia, nor Second-Circle-of-Hellish like Los Angeles. There are automated walkways, a swift and whisper-quiet overhead shuttle train, dozens of bright and cheerful shops and most amazingly, a psychedelic tunnel that connects two main concourses. The glass walls of the tunnel are embedded with LED lights that sparkle and swoop and shift through all the colours of the rainbow and then some, and it's all choreographed to symphonic music. It's a mind blower if you're stone sober. For those who aren't there's a kill switch at both ends of the tunnel that stops the sound and light show for the five minutes necessary to pass through the tunnel. If you want to go on a mild acid trip without ingesting the chemicals, Detroit airport has the venue for you.

I didn't spend a lot of time in Detroit but none of the sights I took in or the people I met suggested I was in a down-and-out city. There's a cocky defiance—a kind of belligerent cheerfulness in the air. The arts and culture scene (perhaps because of the cheap rents) is thriving. Some culturati have taken to calling Detroit "the new Berlin." I passed a sign at the outskirts that read: "Welcome to Detroit, the Renaissance City, Founded 1701."

Detroit's got spunk—and a history of comebacks. It's the only city in North America that's been under the flag of three world powers—French, British and American. It's where Henry Ford built his first car and where the Motown sound was born. You don't know anybody from Detroit? Sure you do. Francis Ford Coppola was born in Detroit. So were Lily Tomlin, Charlton Heston and James Earl Jones. Writers? How about Robert Frost, Elmore Leonard, Joyce Carol Oates?

My favourite Detroit sculpture occupies the middle of a traffic circle near the downtown core. It's a twenty-four-foot bronze of a brown, muscular arm culminating in a forbiddingly clenched human paw.

It's called *The Fist*. It's a homage to Joe Louis, a Detroit native and one of the greatest heavyweight boxers of all time.

Can't imagine a better symbol for Detroit.

And, as Paul Simon pointed out, they do have a helluva hockey team.

Is That You, Jack?

Feature this: a thirty-something Canadian nondescript male toting a backpack lines up to go through security at Vancouver airport. His boarding pass indicates he's heading for Toronto. He plops his backpack on the conveyor belt as instructed, walks through the scanner and prepares to retrieve his bag on the other side.

But his backpack isn't coming through.

Instead the guy at the controls is staring bug-eyed, waving his colleagues over to look at the X-ray image on the screen. In no time an airport security team flanked by a couple of Mounties shows up and escorts the nondescript would-be passenger to the Little Room. They have one question for the guy.

Why is there a loaded, .38-calibre Smith and Wesson revolver and extra rounds of ammunition in his backpack?

I have a larger question for him: what the hell was he thinking?

Is it possible that in this post-9–11, would-be-shoe-bomber and underachieving underpants-detonator era, someone still exists who's bedrock dumb enough to think he could carry a loaded handgun in his carry-on luggage on to an airplane? A police .38 Smith and Wesson is as long as a shoe and weighs a couple of pounds—you're not going to "overlook" it while you're packing and it's difficult to mistake it for a toothbrush.

And those vigilant minions at airport security are positively percolating with paranoia these days. They're confiscating everything from nose-hair tweezers to bobby pins. Last month airport security goons in

Ottawa made headlines by forcing an eighty-five-year-old silver-haired grandmother—four-foot-ten, ninety pounds soaking wet, suffering from osteoporosis and answering to "Cynthia"—to take off her shoes, unzip her pants and submit to a belly prod from an "inspection officer."

Terrorist? No. Terrorized? Definitely.

In Minneapolis a bomb-sniffing dog found a piece of luggage he didn't like. False alarm. Nevertheless, part of the terminal was evacuated. In Portland a Maui-bound flight returned to earth after an overly liquefied passenger turned surly and obnoxious. The airport in Bakersfield, California, was shut down after authorities discovered a "suspicious substance" in a jar in someone's carry-on luggage. It was buckwheat honey.

And this guy tries to board with a .38-calibre revolver in his backpack?

If it's any consolation he's not the only idiot attempting to fly the not-so-friendly skies these days. Mansur Mohammad Assad, a passenger on a Northwest Airways jet bound for Ohio, happened to casually mention that he wanted "to kill all the Jews." That entitled Assad and his 230 fellow passengers to a mid-air U-turn and a quick descent back to Miami airport, escorted by two F-15 fighter jets.

Then there was the forty-two-year-old German dummkopf who was flying with his wife and kids out of Stuttgart last month, heading for a vacation in Egypt. Why not, he apparently thought, have a bit of sport with airport security personnel?

"I have explosives in my underwear," he wittily informed the fraulein wafting the wand.

After they called off the Alsatian attack dogs, let him up off the floor, strip-searched and interrogated him for several hours and thoroughly examined his non-incendiary gotchies, the German airport authorities informed the jokester that not only would he and his family not be flying to Egypt (or anywhere else), they also would not be refunded the cost of their cancelled tickets and would in fact be assessed a thousand-dollar fine plus costs for the entire police operation.

Those airport security people—no sense of humour.

The courts aren't a barrel of laughs these days either. That doofus who tried to fly from Vancouver to Toronto with a pistol in his backpack? He's doing thirty-nine months in the slammer.

There are two lessons to be learned from these current in-flight follies. Number one: If you really have to travel somewhere consider a cab, a bus, a train—hell, duct-tape a bed sheet to your skateboard if you have to—anything but submit to the horrors of commercial air travel these days.

Number two: If you absolutely must fly to somewhere and you spot your old high school buddy Jack Wilson ahead of you in the airport security line-up . . .

Wave at him. Whistle if you like. Semaphore if you know how. Sing your high school anthem if you must.

Just don't yell out "Hi, Jack!"

It's a Jungle out There, Eh?

So there I was, blithely dog-paddling over a tropical reef, my mug immersed in a face mask, a snorkel huffing and spewing just over my right ear. I was admiring the insanely colourful, impossibly beautiful reef fishies flitting and fluttering all around me when I spied something that was . . . the opposite of beautiful. It was mottled brown and grey, about a foot in length and lying partially buried in the sand about five feet beneath the surface of the sea. I was pretty sure it was some kind of life form but it was immobile and strikingly butt-ugly. It looked like a not-very-good potter had started to fashion a fish shape out of inferior clay, found it beyond his powers and abandoned the attempt. I was trying to prod the lump with one of my swim fins when a tiny voice bubbled up in my ear murmuring, "You probably shouldn't mess with that."

When I got ashore I made a sketch of the critter and when I got near an encyclopaedia, I looked it up.

Just as well I hadn't managed to arouse the thing. It was a stone-fish, pound for pound the most venomous fish in the sea. Its dorsal fin features thirteen thorn-sharp, poison-filled spines, each one of which contains enough bad stuff to offer an agonizing death to any creature luckless enough to get jabbed by it.

Well, a tropical climate, what do you expect? It's a jungle out there, bucko. Some equatorial countries feature cockroaches the size of skateboards and enough deadly creepy crawlies to star in their own horror movie.

"Peligro" was one of two words I saw hand-lettered on a sign on a beach near Zihuatenejo, Mexico, years ago. The sign was jammed in the sand in front of a big log. The other word on the sign was "cocodrilo."

"Peligro," I knew, means danger. But "cocodrilo"? Gee, sounds a little bit like "crocodile" . . .

And that's when the log moved its tail.

But you don't have to visit a Spanish-speaking country to find hostile wildlife. Look at Australia—fourteen different types of poisonous snakes, the deadly funnel-web spider, the equally toxic redback spider, plus virulent jellyfish, sea snakes, lionfish, scorpionfish, stinging coral, great white sharks . . .

And oh yeah—crocodiles. Saltwater crocodiles. Up to twenty feet long, a ton and a half heavy, lightning-quick and more than happy to chow down on filet de *Homo sapiens* extra rare whenever they can. Survive all that and you can still get walloped by wallabies, KOd by koala bears or run into a kangaroo capable of punching your lights out.

But the Australian outback pales when compared to India, where you can be eaten by tigers, clawed by leopards, gored by elephants, punctured by cobras and otherwise seriously interfered with by a witches brew of rodents, mammals, reptiles . . .

And insects. You leery about angry hornets? Allow me to introduce you to *Vespa mandarinia*, also known as the Asian giant hornet. How giant? The size of a small bird. The Japanese, who also know the creature, have other names for it. One is "suzume bachi," which translates as "sparrow hornet." The other common name is "yak killer hornet."

Guess how it earned that name.

If Australian wildlife is dangerous, Indian wildlife is a Stephen King novel waiting to be written. Small wonder India suffers a mortality rate that's about thirty times higher than Australia.

Kind of makes you glad you live in a Disneyish, Hobbity unthreatening country like Canada where we plaster our coins with laughing loons and goofy Rudolph reindeer knockoffs and the national mascot is a nearsighted rodent with buckteeth and a pancake tail.

I mentioned (a tad smugly) this innate Great White North superiority to an Aussie friend who's been living in Canada for a few years. He snorted.

"Fair crack o' the whip, myte," he retorted. "You've got a country with polar bears, grizzlies, killer whales, wolverines, rattlesnakes, giant elk, packs of wolves and horny moose with enough armour on their skulls to tip over a car. You've got clouds of bloodsucking deer flies, horseflies, blackflies, no-see-ums and mosquitoes big enough to carry off small children. Safe??? Unthreatening??? Starve the lizards! Give me the outback any day."

He had a point. Several points, actually.

And he hadn't even mentioned Don Cherry.

Ernestine, I Love You

Technology is the knack of organizing the world so that we don't have to experience it.

—MAX FRISCH

So I'm taking this extended road trip down into Washington/ Oregon—the top left-hand corner of America, if you will. It is unfamiliar territory to me. I envision vast carpets of forests and rivers and snow-capped mountain ranges, not to mention unpredictable encounters with hostile grizzlies—some with fur and claws, others with HOMELAND SECURITY on their shoulder flashes and Glock Nines on their hips.

Nervous? Well, maybe a little. I don't know this turf at all and my reputation for finding my way will never get me confused with the likes of Alex Mackenzie or George Vancouver. I can navigate my way through towns and cities okay—even government buildings and department stores—but once the pavement runs out, the street signs disappear and the trees close in, I'm in trouble. To quote Daniel Boone, "I can't say I was ever lost, but I was bewildered once for three days."

So maybe I was a little nervous at the outset of this trip. My pals Brent and Nancy say, "Why don't you borrow our GPS?"

Yeah, right. Me and a new technological gadget. There's a marriage made in Eden.

I don't do modern technology if I can help it. I write on a computer because I can no longer find anyone to repair my ancient hunt 'n peck Olivetti; I tote a cellphone that I never turn on. I don't pack a BlackBerry and no iPod buds plug my aural orifices. I would prefer lathering my naked body in Hellman's mayonnaise for a stroll through a mosquito-infested bog to tackling something as mind-bending and complicated as a portable Global Positioning System. On the other hand I don't want to look any stupider in front of my friends than I already do. I accept their GPS. They show me how it mounts on a little bracket that attaches to the windshield. All I have to do is plug it into the car cigarette lighter and I'm in business, they assure me.

Fine, fine—just gimme the damn thing. I figure I'll stuff it under the front seat, make the trip my usual way, with Rand-McNally maps flapping like pterodactyls all over the car, then give them back their fur-shlugginer GPS when I return. "Couldn't get it to work," I'd tell them. "Must need a new battery or something."

But somewhere along the road I look over and notice Ernestine.

I don't always pick up hitchhikers but she was hard to resist. Sleek and sassy, trim and elegant, I was in love from the first words she uttered:

"MAKE SLIGHT LEFT TURN IN POINT FIVE KILOMETRES," she purred.

It was true! There WAS a left turn in half a kilometre! How could she know that?

The rest of the trip was a piece of cake. With Ernestine up front with me I breezed through Seattle, Portland, the Olympic Mountains, the coastal switchbacks. Ernestine's been everywhere and she's got a photographic memory. She can tell you where to find a movie house, a historical monument, a bank or gas station.

Restaurants? No problem. Did you want Thai or Taco Bell? Five-star or drive-thru? Ernestine knows 'em all. "TURN RIGHT ON I-95 IN SIX POINT FIVE KILOMETRES," cooed my travelling companion. She definitely pressed my buttons.

Or rather, I pressed hers. Ernestine wasn't flesh and blood. She was—is—a three-inch-by-six-inch slab of computer technology that sits above my dashboard and leads me from home to destination and back in a sultry, imperturbable voice. She has an American accent—she says "AVEN-OO" for "avenue" and "RA-OWT" for "route"—and she has this cute lisp that suggests she might have sipped a glass of wine before she went on duty.

But mortal she ain't. Ernestine is a Magellan RoadMate 1440 Global Positioning gizmo. I named her in honour of Lily Tomlin's famous telephone operator—although in truth my Ernestine is much, much nicer.

Ernestine and her constantly updating 3-D route display transforms a road trip in ways I could never have imagined. Ernestine banishes travel angst. She makes driving fun again. Even when I screw up Ernestine is cool and composed. If I drive past a turnoff or overshoot a light she doesn't groan or have a fit or crumple up the map and stare out the window like, er, some people I could mention. Ernestine simply murmurs calmly "AS SOON AS POSSIBLE, MAKE A LEGAL U-TURN."

I have a pal who has another name for his GPS. "Cindy and I call it 'the marital aid,'" he says. "I can't guess how many times it's saved our marriage on the road."

True enough. Best of all, even the wife loves Ernestine.

Foist, We Take Manhattan

It is an ugly city, a dirty city. Its climate is a scandal. Its politics are used to frighten children. Its traffic is madness. Its competition is murderous. But . . . once you have lived in New York and it has become your home, no other place is good enough.

—JOHN STEINBECK

Ah, yes . . . Noo Yawk, Noo Yawk. Back in the 1980s *Toronto Star* columnist Michele Landsberg spent a few years living in New York while her husband Stephen Lewis served as Canada's ambassador to the United Nations. She got her Big Apple baptism on Fifth Avenue one afternoon after hailing a taxi. Landsberg was about to climb in the back seat when a stout, mink-coated matron blindsided her, body-checked her out of the way and commandeered the cab.

"B-b-b-but this is MY taxi," Landsberg stammered. The matron snarled, "This is Noo Yawk, honey!" and slammed the door.

Yep, New Yorkers have brass dangly bits, no doubt about it. As George Segal said, "In New York there's no room for amateurs, even in crossing the streets."

And as far as New York taxis go, Johnny Carson said it best: "Any time four New Yorkers get into a cab together without arguing, a bank robbery has just taken place."

New Yorkers are world famous, and nothing says "New Yorker" like the accent. "Water" becomes "wawtuh," "doctor" becomes "dawktuh." A New Yorker doesn't park his car, he "pahks" his "cah." And an inquiry as to whether or not one has dined becomes a masterpiece of minimalism: "Jeet?" "No—Jew?"

There is probably no better-known accent in the world. Think Edith Bunker: "Awww c'man, Awwwchie." Think Tony Soprano: "Whaddyagonnadoo?" The accent—like just about everything else in New York—is defiant, up front and in your face.

And some New Yorkers spend thousands of bucks to get rid of it.

Really. According to a story in the *New York Times* there are more than a dozen businesses in Manhattan dedicated to teaching their customers not to sound like they come from New York.

Why would a Gothamite want to lose the most recognized accent in the world? Because they think it's "unrefined." It sounds, as a Brit might say, "common." Lynn Singer, a speech therapist with several New York clients, is blunter. "A New York accent makes you sound ignorant," she told the *Times* reporter. Presumably therapists like Ms. Singer can take the rough edges off a person's speaking style, sand it down, backfill the glottal potholes, tighten up the diphthongs and all in all make a New Yorker sound like he or she comes from . . . well, nowhere, actually.

Don't laugh, it's a trend. I have actor friends in Vancouver and Toronto who are paying good money to voice coaches in order to "lose" their Canadian accent. They think a homogenized, unrecognizable speech pattern will help get them work in American television and theatre.

Perhaps it will—but it sucks.

I appreciate hearing Prairie twang or West Coast mellow in a person's voice. I enjoy figuring out whether I'm talking to a Yukoner or a Bluenoser, a James Bay Cree from Ontario or a Plains Cree from Calgary. Canada is a tossed salad of regional accents—staccato bursts of Quebecois, the Gaelic lilt of Cape Bretoners, the Dickensian cadences of the Newfoundland outports, to name just a few. There is a drive to flatten out all that glorious diversity, to make us all sound like Lloyd Robertson and I hope it fails.

Ah, but do accents really matter? New Yorker Mary Ellen Orchard thinks so. She explained why her accent is important in a letter to the editor:

"As a person who grew up in Manhattan, then moved to Queens, then moved to Long Island, by the second sentence of our introduction you will know that I am decisive, direct, funny, warm, don't tolerate fools and will feed you a fabulous meal and welcome you into my home at a moment's notice for as long as you need.

"And what is your accent telling me? Your accent is telling me nothing at all."

Think Mary Ellen Orchard will be attending an "accent eradication" course anytime soon?

Fuggeddaboudit.

Have a Nice Fright

On our way to the airport to catch a flight to San Francisco recently I subjected my sweetie to a few lines from the poem *High Flight*:

"O I have slipped the surly bonds of earth," I intoned,
"And danced the skies on laughter-silvered wings.
Sunward I've climbed, and joined the sun-split clouds
And done a hundred things you have not dreamed of . . . "

I recited those lines to rekindle my appreciation for the sheer glory and wonder of the flying experience—the miracle that a wingless, gravity-burdened biped like me can actually soar above the clouds higher than an eagle, swifter than a peregrine falcon . . .

And to prepare us for the fact that the flight we were about to take would probably not be glorious, wonderful or miraculous. It would more likely be stressful, uncomfortable and slightly crazy making.

I was right.

It began at the check-in desk where the Gorgon in charge cast an appraising eye over our two suitcases. "You are aware," she smirked, "that United Airlines now charges twenty-five dollars for each piece of checked luggage?"

No. No, we were not aware of that. I guess we just assumed that the obscenely inflated price of the airline tickets included a piece of checked baggage for each passenger, the way it has since, oh, the days of Wilbur and Orville Wright.

We fork over $50 we had hoped to spend in San Francisco.

Then there was the security shakedown. I was lucky—I only had to remove my hat, empty my pockets, undo my belt and take my shoes off. My sweetie got all that plus a humiliatingly intimate hand frisk from two Stalinesque Amazons who didn't trouble to hide the fact that they were Not Having a Good Day.

"With a grope like that I was expecting a marriage proposal," muttered my sweetie.

But I didn't get angry. Not even when the check-in goon pounced like a mongoose on my tiny money clip. It has (had) an (I swear to the gods) inch-long nail file I'd forgotten was even there. A nail file. An inch long. You'd think they'd apprehended a Taliban grenade launcher or a Turkish scimitar at least. "That can't go on," said the jut-jawed security guy. "Keep it," I told him. My Number One rule for air travel: Never, ever lose your cool going through security. That only leads to a World of Pain.

Not that an aura of Zen-like equanimity will protect you from trauma in the flight that follows. You still have to wedge yourself into the Lilliputian seating accommodation in which you spend the flight inhaling the hair oil of the passenger in front of you while the edge of your "chair table" cuts off circulation to your lower body.

I have breaking news on that particular feature of air travel: it's about to get even worse.

An Italian company called Aviointeriors is flogging a new . . . well, aircraft "seat" is not quite the word—it's a kind of saddle that passengers would be expected to straddle leaving them in a half-sitting, half-standing position for the duration of their flight.

They're calling it the Skyrider. Prospective passengers have been understandably cool toward the Skyrider but airline executives are salivating all over their pinstripe vests. Why? Legroom, baby. The Skyrider not only weighs less than half of normal airline seats, it offers only 58.4 centimetres of legroom compared to the grotesquely wasteful 76.2 centimetres passengers currently receive. Result: a plane full of Skyrider "seats" can cram in 14 percent more human meat than a conventional plane.

Ever wondered what it feels like to be a factory farm chicken? Looks like air travellers are about to find out.

I can think of one or two improvements airlines might make before they invest in Skyrider squat seats. They could give us tray tables that actually work instead of the flimsy wafers that buck your coffee up in your face at the first whiff of air turbulence.

They could give us actual armrests wide enough for the two forearms that are supposed to share them.

How about some real smiles? Cutting back on the canned announcements? Some actual fresh air? How about treating us like actual paying customers instead of just so many units of unruly freight?

How about just being honestly pleasant?

Yeah, right. When pigs fly.

Big Brother is Watching Us

Here's a story for our times: An American citizen is confronted by police officers, guns drawn, in New York City. She is handcuffed and taken into custody where she is detained and questioned for several hours. Ultimately she is released.

Her crime? Doodling. On her school desk. The would-be felon is Alexa Gonzalez, a twelve-year-old elementary school student. She had written—in erasable ink—"I LOVE MY FRIENDS ABBY AND FAITH. She then signed it: LEX WAS HERE, 2/1/10.

Police??? Handcuffs????

School officials later allowed that perhaps Alexa's arrest was a mistake. "Based on what we've seen so far," said a school official, "this shouldn't have happened."

Well, duh.

We live in paranoid times. The same newspaper that carried the tale of Alexa's run-in with the Keystone Kops in New York ran a story of a similar happening a little closer to home. That story concerned the mass evacuation of a public school in Saanich, north of Victoria, BC.

Not so surprising, really. Saanich lies on the dreaded fault line along which seismologists assure us a major earthquake will occur sooner or later. Perhaps a tremor had shivered through the school auditorium? Or maybe there'd been a cougar sighting? Or a serial killer alert?

Nope. What triggered the mass evacuation of students was a note discovered in a girls' washroom that contained "threatening language." Classes were suspended, school buses were summoned, students and faculty took the rest of the day off while a full police investigation was launched. Over a piece of paper in a girls' washroom.

Times change. I remember back in my public school days when a fellow student named Ivan "went postal." Ivan was a tough cookie even in grade eight and he had a lot of energy to burn off. On this particular day he chose to chill out by punching out the lower windows in one of the school portables. He was pretty good at it. I think he did twelve or thirteen before Mr. Creighton, the shop teacher, grabbed him by the scruff of his shirt and hauled him off to the school nurse.

Schools handled "threats" differently then. The nurse stitched Ivan up, the principal kicked him out of school, his parents got a bill for the broken windows and the rest of us didn't even get the afternoon off.

I can't imagine what might happen to Ivan if he tried that stunt today—particularly if he chose an airport in which to "act out."

Consider the case of Jules Paul Bouloute. Mr. Bouloute is a fifty-seven-year-old Haitian who had just come from his devastated homeland, landed at Kennedy Airport and in the noise and confusion, not to mention signage in a foreign language, made the mistake of a lifetime.

Mr. Bouloute attempted to go through the wrong door.

It was only an emergency exit that would have put Mr. Bouloute back on the tarmac but the airport officials responded as if the man's underpants had exploded. Sirens whooped, alarms blared, security staff scrambled and deployed, and Mr. Bouloute was, of course, arrested. He's lucky he wasn't tasered into a crispy critter. That can happen at airports these days.

Well, perhaps not so lucky. Mr. Bouloute was tackled and shackled, then arraigned on charges of first-degree criminal tampering and third-degree criminal trespass. He faces, as of this writing, up to seven years in prison.

Can't you hear the conversation in the prison exercise yard?

"What you in for, man?"

"Murder."

"Bank job."

"Assault with a weapon."

"How about you, buddy?"

"Um, I tried to go through the wrong door . . . "

As a not unrelated aside, I got an email from my old pal Krieno this week. Krieno and I went to journalism school together many moons ago. "Do you recall," he wrote, "when we carefully stuck a lit cigarette onto the fuse of a cherry bomb,* placed it in a locker outside the cafeteria, then retired to our favourite lunch table to await the inevitable outcome? The explosion bent the locker door and happened, as luck would have it, at the exact moment the dean of journalism walked by with a delegation of visitors. Today, such a stunt would undoubtedly bring the full force of the law streaming onto the campus . . . and we'd be doing six to ten on a terrorism charge."

Indeed. We might even be sharing a cell with Monsieur Bouloute.

(*cherry bomb: a sort of firecracker on steroids)

Been There, Got the T-shirt

I'm sleeping with a woman in Corsica.

Not from Corsica—in Corsica. What's more, her husband is in bed with us. He doesn't suspect a thing.

It's . . . complicated.

For one thing, I am not—worse luck—actually in Corsica myself. I am in snow-bound Canada, typing at a kitchen table with a scarf around my neck. But my avatar, my Doppelganger, my other self, is down there in Corsica, enjoying the ocean breeze that's wafting through the open window and over the, er, three of us.

It's like this: Once upon a time I had a radio show called *Basic Black* that ran on the CBC—the Canadian Broadcasting Corporation. One day a slick-looking dude from the PR department buttonholed me in the CBC cafeteria. "We'd like to do some advertising for your show," he purred. Swell, I said.

"We were thinking of T-shirts," he said. Okay, I said.

"What would you like on the T-shirt?" he asked me. "Uh . . . the name of the show?" I guessed. He shook his head sadly, as if he was dealing with a slow-learning Labrador. "We'll need more than that," he said.

We kicked it around for a while. He rejected the idea of snappy slogans, funny quotes or a staff photo. My coffee was getting cold. "How about I draw a cartoon of myself?" I suggested. "Perfect," he said.

That's how we ended up with 147 cartons of *Basic Black* T-shirts emblazoned with a cartoon head depicting a bald guy with a big nose and a straggly beard grinning crookedly above my scrawled signature. The cartoon is laughably amateurish and looks, if I may say so, unlike any human alive.

Everybody says it's a perfect likeness.

That was my first embarrassment—everybody who saw the gargoyle I'd scrawled immediately knew it was me. But worse—it became (unlike any of my books) an immediate bestseller.

We couldn't keep it in stock. In a matter of weeks the *Basic Black* T-shirt was showing up on the torsos of loggers in Prince George, wheat farmers in the Prairies, secretaries on Bay Street, oyster-shuckers in Lunenburg and (I know—I saw the photo) on a co-ed quartet of skiers schussing down the side of a mountain near Invermere, BC.

Who, aside from ski boots, appear to be wearing nothing BUT their *Basic Black* T-shirts.

Well, that's the thing about this garment—it only comes in one colour (black, natch) and as an extra cost-cutting measure the PR department decided we would order it in just one size: extra large.

If you're built like Arnold Schwarzenegger (or for that matter like an Amazon with breast implants)—it's a perfect fit. Otherwise, you've got pyjamas.

That's how I came to be sleeping with that woman in Corsica. "I'm wearing my *Basic Black* T-shirt to bed tonight," she wrote on a postcard.

I suppose, technically, I'm sleeping with hundreds of women right now, when you think about it. Thousands, maybe.

Well . . . dozens, for sure.

But it's no bed of roses. The husband of that Corsican correspondent I mentioned? I hear that he's . . . wearing me too.

I told you—it's complicated.

Portland Here I Come

I'm not a city slicker, I'm a country mouse. If I have to be in a city I prefer Victoria—mostly because it isn't much of a city. The people there are still friendly, the buildings don't blot out the sun. It's still easy to scoot around the infrequent traffic jams and you hardly ever see a drive-by shooting.

In addition to being a rustic I'm a homer. Ever since that bloated monster called Homeland Security threw its paranoid pall over US border crossings I exit Canada southward as seldom as possible. That said, I've just discovered my second favourite city and it makes my short list even though it involves a border crossing. The city is Portland, Oregon, an eight-hour train ride, five-hour drive or a one-hour flight south of Vancouver. About six hundred thousand Portlanders have settled at the confluence of the Willamette and Columbia rivers and a fine job they've done of the place, all things considered. It's hard to get lost in Portland because the city is neatly divided into four quadrants. The Willamette River cleaves east Portland from west Portland; Burnside Street does the same between north and south.

If you do get turned around just look to the horizon. Portland sits on an ancient lava bed. It's surrounded by twenty-four peaks and mountains including Mount St. Helens, which spectacularly blew its top thirty years ago. Easy to orient yourself; even easier to get around Portland once you do. They have clean, wide, pothole-free streets, an abundance of cabs and bike paths and a public transit system that's the envy of the world.

So what kind of itch can you scratch in Portland? To paraphrase Marlon the biker, "Whaddya got?"

Music? Live performances of everything from jazz to garage rock, classical to punk.

Great restaurants, plenty of museums and art galleries, an actual 5,000-acre wilderness park within the city limits. Portland also has the goofily named but amazingly vibrant International Rose Test Garden, featuring more varieties of the love flower than you can imagine and explaining why Portland calls itself the City of Roses.

Thirsty? One of Portland's other nicknames is Beervana, thanks to the plethora of microbreweries and brewpubs that abound. If you lean to caffeine you'll find more coffee houses, cafés and micro-roasteries than you can shake a packet of Sweet 'n Low at.

And then there's Powell's. The world's biggest bookstore, new and used, bestsellers and obscure rarities. An entire city block, so huge they hand you a map when you go through the door. If you like books Powell's is reason enough to visit Portland.

But there's something else about the city that I couldn't put my finger on at first. Portland . . . just feels different. Like no other US city I've ever visited. Everyone's polite, citizens aren't yelling into their cellphones or chatting at 110 decibels. There's no trash on the streets. And there's a distinct lack of the usual patriotic flag waving. The city of Portland isn't very . . . American. It's more like . . . Canada. One of its funkiest neighbourhoods, full of boutiques, cafés and galleries, is called the Alberta Arts District. Which is just across the river from . . . Fort Vancouver.

I don't think any American city has felt this Canadian since our troops marched in and burned the Washington White House in the War of 1812.

Not that it feels like an occupied city—on the contrary. Portland is free and easy, accessible and friendly. And just about the last place in North America where you'd ever run into, say Dick Cheney. Or Rush Limbaugh.

Two pretty decent reasons to visit the city right there.

Rent a White Guy

You looking for work? Have I got a job for you. The starting pay is fairly decent—a thousand bucks a week, tax free—and there's a ton of travel involved. You'll fly business class to foreign destinations, get put up in first-class hotels and chow down in five-star restaurants. Best of all there's no experience necessary. All you need to qualify is a present-able pair of shoes, a white shirt, tie and a half-decent business suit.

It would probably be better if you're not sporting nose rings, a Mohawk hairdo or a BORN TO RAISE HELL tattoo on your forehead but other than that, you're good to go.

Providing you're also a white guy.

Rent a White Guy—it's the latest craze in China where industrial towns and cities are exploding like cancer cells. Factories and office buildings take root and blossom overnight. For some inscrutable reason Chinese entrepreneurs have concluded that having white guys—pretty much any white guys—hanging around adds prestige to their opera-tions. Such employees do not have to have any industrial expertise or training. All they have to do is show up and . . . look pale. Canadian journalist Mitch Moxley described his recent experience as a White Guy rental in an article on theatlantic.com.

He was met at the Beijing airport and given the details of his job—representing a US-based company building a facility in the city of Dongying. He would be required to make trips to the construction site, attend a ribbon-cutting and rub shoulders with the Chinese.

And that's it! Don't speak Mandarin? No problem. Haven't got a clue about the company you're theoretically representing? Fuggeddaboudit. Just show up and . . . be a white guy. They'll even have personalized business cards (in Chinese, of course) printed up and waiting for you.

I'd be inclined to dismiss the story as an Oriental Urban Legend if it wasn't for the experiences of my nephew in Japan. Said nephew—let's call him Paddy to protect the guilty—spent a few years in Japan as a young student. Paddy could hardly have chosen a culture he was less likely to blend into physically. He looks like a Viking hero action figure, tall, broad-shouldered, blonde and blue-eyed.

Whereas your average Japanese male is . . . not.

But far from being a disadvantage Paddy's white guy-ishness conveyed a kind of instant celebrity. Strangers gaped and smiled spontaneously. Japanese families asked to have their pictures taken with him. He grew accustomed to being treated as something between a freak of nature and a Hollywood star (if, in fact, there's any difference). The more adventurous Japanese girls were thrilled to help him, um, practise his Japanese. For a single guy, life was good.

And then it got better. Paddy was approached by a Japanese firm and asked if he would like to become a marriage priest. Religious affiliation? Not important. Command of the Japanese language? No problem—there would be a script. Besides, his less than perfect white-guy accent was . . .

Exactly what they wanted.

Turns out there are considerable cultural brownie points to be gained among certain Japanese by having a certified White Guy oversee their marriage vows. For the better part of three years Paddy would receive a phone call once or twice a week instructing him to be at such and such a pagoda at such and such a time. Sometimes the calls would come at almost the last minute, resulting in Paddy haring across Tokyo on his motor scooter, his priestly robes billowing out behind him.

The sight caused a few Japanese "salarymen" to swear off the sake forever.

It was a sweet gig. Excellent pay, minimal hours and no heavy lifting. Then there was the time it didn't work so well. Paddy was halfway through the ceremony, the about-to-be newlyweds kneeling blissfully before him. He was intoning the vows from the script before him when, unaccountably, the pages stuck to each other.

"I skipped over two or three pages of the ceremony altogether," Paddy recalls. He didn't yet comprehend Japanese well enough to catch his error and the bride and groom were either too in love or too nervous to notice the boo-boo, but folks in the bridal party sensed something was out of whack. Complaints were lodged with Paddy's employer.

Paddy's not sure what the upshot was—he's not even sure the couple is technically married. "I think maybe they got a discount or something," he says.

Good lesson for Paddy. He boned up on his Japanese to make sure such a mistake wouldn't happen again.

Good lesson for the bride and groom too: don't expect the course of true love to run smooth just because some white guy is in charge.

Spread Your Tiny Wings!

Of all the odd names our country's known by—the Great White North, Canuckistan, Hoser Heaven, America's Toque—I think "Land of the Snowbird" is the most enchanting.

What's not to like about a snowbird? Whether it's a reference to the song immortalized by Anne Murray or a skyward salute to the crack Canadian Forces air squadron that flies out of CFB Moose Jaw, snowbirds are as quintessentially Canadian as, well, Anne Murray and Moose Jaw.

We are all snowbirds up here, if not in deed, at least in our dreams. From spring to fall we feed and nest and raise our broods and chirrup chattily across the land and then suddenly, in the chill nether months of the calendar, we spontaneously coalesce into jittery flocks and migrate south. Or sometimes east or west—anywhere, really, that affords respite from at least a couple of week's worth of Canadian winter

When the snow starts to fly we do too. We head for the US, mostly, but we also export sizeable clumps of weather-leery refugees to Cuba and Mexico, the UK and France. One thing virtually all of our international destinations have in common: they're warmer than downtown Winnipeg in January.

As a writer and gypsy wannabe I've bounced around the globe a fair bit but not nearly enough. There are still plenty of exotic destinations on my bucket list.

Bad trips? I've had a few. I've been Down in the Dumps, Under the Weather and Behind the Eight Ball—even Close to Tears, Around the

Bend and Next to Impossible. But I've also been High as a Kite and Over the Moon. Sure, I've been In the Red—but I've also been In the Pink. I've been Driven to Distraction, travelled from the Sublime to the Ridiculous and, as an Aeroplan card-carrying snowbird, I've more than once Flown into a Tizzy.

Here in Snowbirdland I've checked into hostelries in Spuzzum and Horsefly in BC but I have yet to lay my head in Saint-Louis-du-Ha! Ha! Quebec or Punkeydoodles Corners in Ontario. I've barhopped in Flin Flon, Manitoba, and strolled through Head-Smashed-In Buffalo Jump in Alberta. I've dogsledded in Pukaskwa Park and chugalugged a Sourtoe Cocktail (don't ask) in Dawson City, Yukon. Peggy's Cove? Been there, got the T-shirt. New Brunswick? Am I likely to pass up a province that boasts a Blacks Harbour AND a Blackville?

The only province I haven't done justice to is Newfoundland and Labrador. That's because, frankly, I feel sexually intimidated by that cod-forsaken corner of the country. I still remember that *Maclean's* magazine poll a few years back declaring Newfoundlanders enjoy sex more often than any other Canadians. Well, big surprise. Look at the place names they grow up with: Dildo? Blow Me Down? Cupids? Conception Bay? Heart's Desire, Delight and Content? I'm surprised Hugh Hefner didn't move the entire Playboy empire to Come By Chance years ago.

Is Newfoundland on my bucket list? Of course it is— I'm a snowbird, eh? I'll be dropping by one of these (summer) days.

But not without a preparatory side trip to Viagara Falls.

Zip to My Lou, My Darlin'

"A zip line, also known as a Tyrolean crossing or death slide, consists of a pulley suspended on a cable mounted on an incline." That's what my dictionary says about zip-lining. My attention wavered right after the phrase "death slide." The idea of whooshing through a forest canopy past carcass-impaling conifers, across canyons, between boulders and over boiling cataracts protected only by a doggie leash hooked to a stainless steel wire sounded nuts to me. Only a juvenile, testosterone-ridden, Evel Knievel clone would entertain the idea of zip-lining.

"We should try zip-lining," says my pal, Lou.

I don't know where Lou gets these ideas. We are both "of an age" at which mature contemplation and serene detachment are the norm. Let younger fools man the ramparts, headman the puck, run back the punt return, gallop to the vanguard. We who are older and wiser get to watch and advise from the sidelines.

"Says here it's only ninety bucks for a whole afternoon," says Lou. "That's a good deal."

I explain to Lou that zip-lining is a young man's pursuit. I point out that as aging adults our reflexes are slower, our bodies more reluctant to heal. I ask Lou to consider how long it would take an ambulance with paramedics and a body board to even *find* us out there in the wilderness.

"I'll pick up two tickets for Saturday," says Lou.

Lou gets a little hard of hearing when it's convenient. Like the time we all tried to talk Lou out of getting tattooed. "Kid stuff, Lou!" we said. Couldn't hear us. Got a tattoo of a butterfly, for god's sake. On the shoulder.

Same thing with the whitewater rafting in Alaska. And riding the elephant in Delhi and the camel in Cairo. When Lou decides to do something, Lou does it.

Which is how I came to find myself decked out in a helmet and safety goggles, trussed into a diaper-like harness halfway up a Douglas fir on a Vancouver Island mountainside.

With Lou helmeted and diapered, right beside me.

We had spent half an hour bumping up the mountainside in Jeep 4X4s and the rest of the afternoon coming back down on zip lines, zinging, snakes-and-ladders style, on a series of cables. Some were high—up to 150 feet above the ground. Some were long—over 1,000 feet in one case. All of them were quite "zippy"—they say we reached speeds of sixty-five kilometers per hour at one point. I wouldn't know. My eyes, like all other orifices, were clenched shut.

But Lou was right. It was thrilling—and eerily quiet, with only the zing of the zip line and the whistle of wind in the ears.

Oh yes, and the sound of Lou ululating like Pavarotti. I came whizzing in to the final stop whimpering quietly, curled in a fetal ball. Not Lou. Lou came in legs pinwheeling, chest-thumping like a superannuated ape man. All the other zip-liners gave Lou a standing ovation on touchdown. Fair enough. Lou earned it.

Did I mention Lou is eighty-three?

Did I mention Lou's first name is Betty?

You go, girl.

PART THREE

Hi-tech, Lo-tech, No-tech

Haven't Had a Bath in Years

I have had a good many more uplifting thoughts, creative and expansive visions while soaking in comfortable baths than I have ever had in any cathedral.

—EDMUND WILSON

Ah, the pleasures of the bath. It didn't take humankind very long to cotton on to the luxury of a leisurely soak in an oversized bucket of unusually warm water. The Japanese and Turks figured it out a few centuries ago. For ancient Greeks and Romans a sojourn at the public baths was frequently the social highlight of the day.

And today? Sorry, too busy. Public baths are quaint, bordering on extinct. Filling a tub just for oneself is too finicky, environmentally wasteful and takes far too long. There's just enough time for a quick spritz under the showerhead and then it's back to the rat race.

We used to surrender to the pleasure of "drawing a bath." Now it's more like a NASCAR pit stop. Bathtubs have become something you try not to slip in while showering.

That helps to explain why bathtubs are disappearing. Rooms in Holiday Inns used to have tubs in every bathroom. From now on only 55 percent of their new hotel rooms will feature tubs.

It's a trend. Marriot Hotels forecasts that soon 75 percent of the rooms they rent will be "showers only." "Most business people are on the run and take a quick shower," says Marriot vice-president Bill Barrie. "There's no time for baths."

I tsk-tsk this development, strictly on principle, you understand. The fact is I haven't had a bath in years.

It's not that I'm a big shower fan or a time-management fanatic—
it's just that the bathtub ain't what it used to be. I grew up with those
massive, cast-iron, water-guzzling claw-foot tubs that occupied an entire
wall of the bathroom. They took ten minutes to fill but you wound up
reclining like a sultan with the water up to your lower lip. The hot and
cold water taps were down by your feet and they had big knurly knobs
on them, the better to be manipulated—make that "toe-nipulated"—to
keep the water piping hot. It was pretty ingenious and delightful as
human inventions go. And then some designer fool came along and
decided that bathtubs weren't svelte enough. They went plastic, lowered the profile, squinched up the dimensions and added water jets and
moulded soap dishes. The result? The modern bathtub. Once you've
folded in your legs and hunched in your torso you're lucky if the water
level reaches your navel.

Much nicer lines than the old claw foot of course; a sexier silhouette
I suppose—but a lousier experience.

The irony is, psychologists are discovering that people actually *need*
the pleasures of a hot bath—need it, in fact, even more than we used to.
Researchers at Yale studied 400 people between the ages of eighteen and
sixty-five and discovered that modern folks use hot baths and showers as
a way to connect with, not escape from, the world around them.

"The lonelier we get, the more we substitute the missing social
warmth with physical warmth," says psychologist John Bargh. "We
don't know why we're doing it, but it helps."

Well, no offence, Dr. Bargh, but I know why we're doing it—
because it harms no one, won't frighten the horses, contains no calories
and feels fabulous.

A lot cheaper than a pricey odyssey with a psychoanalyst too.
Nobody put it better than Susan Glassee, who wrote: "I can't think of
any sorrow that a hot bath wouldn't help just a little bit."

Amen to that. Alas, I fear the glory days of the real bathtub are
behind it. Nearly a century and a half behind, to be precise. The modern
bathtub was invented in 1850.

Alexander Graham Bell made the first telephone call to Watson, his
assistant, in 1875.

Just think.

There were twenty-five glorious years when you could soak in the
tub without having the phone ring.

Phony as a Three-Dollar Bill

A story I heard at my pappy's knee post-Second World War went like this: One day circa 1940 the Nazi High Command was sitting around discussing ways to destroy Great Britain. The Blitzkrieg bombers were being turned back by the RAF. The V-2 rockets were only sporadically successful. Panzer troops were too overextended for a cross-Channel invasion. How about, someone suggested, blanketing the British Isles with counterfeit money—ten-, twenty-, even fifty-pound notes as perfectly fabricated as German technology could concoct, so fiendishly accurate even monetary experts couldn't detect them?

The story went that Himmler shook his head and murmured "No. That would be too cruel."

The story was, of course, as phony as a three-dollar bill. Nothing (certainly not an illicit printing job) was too cruel for those arch thugs of the twentieth century. In fact the Nazis did launch an elaborate plot to blanket Great Britain with impeccable quality bogus British currency. We'll never know how devastating the scheme might have been because: (a) the Brits got wind of it; and (b) the Nazis were defeated before it was fully mobilized.

In any case Nazis were Johan-come-latelies in the forgery biz. Common crooks have been tinkering with currency and tampering with coinage pretty much since money was invented nearly three millennia ago.

Nations have tried their hand at forgery before as well. The Brits cranked out fake Continental dollars to hamstring the Americans during the Revolutionary War; the US Feds did it to the Confederate South in the American Civil War. Ironically, the Feds blew it. The bogus Confederate currency they manufactured was easily recognizable because it was infinitely superior to the "real" thing.

Government counterfeiting still goes on. North Korea—which, if it were a dog, would be declared rabid—turns out virtually no agricultural or industrial commodities for the world's markets. What it does produce are illicit drugs, fake Viagra and sheets and sheets of fake American hundred-dollar bills. Very good ones. Kim Jong Un's mob employs top-of-the-line Swiss-made intaglio printing presses that only governments can purchase. North Korean diplomats and other toadies then pass the bills at overseas racetracks, casinos and other venues that accept large bills without question. American authorities estimate that over the past number of years North Korea has slipped over $1 billion worth of fake American currency into the world's financial bloodstream.

Not that counterfeit money always has to be sophisticated. Police in Greensburg, Pennsylvania, recently arrested a woman for "theft by deception" after she paid for some clothes at a Fashion Bug store—with an American $200 bill.

You know—the one with George Bush on the front? And the legend on the back that reads "We Like Broccoli"?

As a forgery the bill was just slightly more high tech than Monopoly money. A spokesman said that police were "unsure" how a clerk could be taken in by it.

And here in Canada? A couple of weeks ago I got up to the cashier at a supermarket with a buggy full of groceries, laid them on the conveyor belt and presented the cashier with a Canadian $100 bill.

"We don't take those," sniffed the cashier.

"What do you mean?" I said. "I just got this from my Credit Union. Read the small print. It says, 'Bank of Canada. This is legal tender.'"

My cashier shrugged loquaciously. Final score: grocery store one, Black, nil. Fortunately I'm a generous man who doesn't hold grudges. I even let them put all my groceries back on their shelves.

Later I checked with a Mountie and she told me that a lot of Canadian businesses routinely refuse to accept Canadian $50 and $100 bills these days. It's probably because of a huge counterfeiting ring that operated for a few months near Windsor, Ontario, back in 2001, pumping millions of dollars worth of fake fifties and hundreds into the economy.

As for my shopping impasse, it could have been worse, I suppose. Back in the mid-1990s German police arrested a guy on his way to our shores with nearly $11 million worth of counterfeit Canadian currency in his knapsack.

Make that counterfeit Canadian Tire currency.

I'm glad the cops nailed him before he got to a Canadian Tire outlet on this side of the pond.

With my luck I'd have been standing in line behind him at the checkout.

Th-Th-Th-That's Balls, Folks!

Ever heard of "The Celebrated Jumping Frog of Calaveras County"? It's the title of the story that made Mark Twain famous. America's Dean of Humour wrote it for a weekly paper in 1865 when he was a thirty-year-old itinerant bumming his way around the American west. It's a tall tale about an inveterate gambler who'd lay a wager on anything. One day he bets a stranger that his pet frog can jump higher than the stranger's can. The gambler loses the bet—even though his frog is known as a champion jumper. Why? Because when he wasn't looking the stranger poured a quarter pound of lead buckshot down the champion frog's throat.

Lucky for Mr. Twain he wrote that story nearly a century and a half ago. If he published it today he'd be famous all over again but for all the wrong reasons. He'd be outed on Facebook as a callous enabler and slammed by PETA for cruelty to animals.

When it comes to the interaction of people and animals times have changed, as the people of Ailsa Craig could tell you. Although it sounds like the name of an Advice to the Lovelorn columnist, Ailsa Craig is a sleepy little village not far from London, Ontario. Each year at their summer festival Ailsa Craigians sponsor a turtle race. They've been doing it for over thirty years. Kids go out and find painted turtles that, in season, roam freely all over town, take them home and "train" them (it's like herding tomcats), then enter them in the one-day, once-a-year "race" at the summer fair. The turtles straggle toward the finish line, a winner is declared then all the turtles are plopped back in the river.

"These turtle races are a tradition," says Laurie Rees, one of the event organizers, "a way for families to get together."

Well, not any more they aren't. The Ministry of Natural Resources recently informed festival organizers that they were breaking the law. It is illegal to hunt or harbour any wild turtle in Ontario. Draconian? Perhaps not. We humans have grown accustomed to treating the other inhabitants of this orb with a kind of arrogant contempt. We throw baited hooks in the water, blow ducks out of the air, put canaries in cages, blast away at deer and elk and moose and bear and don't think a whole lot about the morality of it all. I remember seeing some kids in a local park tossing a small grass snake back and forth. I told them to stop. Their mother huffed up, looked at me like I was some kind of sentimental fool and hissed, "It's only a snake!"

Which brings us to the Calgary Stampede. Call me unpatriotic but I don't get off on this annual spectacle either. Oh, I have no problem with a celebration that encourages city geeks to wear goofy hats, talk like Yosemite Sam and dress up like extras from the Village People, but the animal toll is getting hard to ignore. One year six horses died. Two had heart attacks, one broke its back during a bucking event, two were so badly injured they had to be euthanized. The year before that the death count was three horses and a steer, which suffered a spinal cord injury during a roping competition.

Let's see now: you cattle prod a terrified steer into galloping across a corral, throw a lasso around its neck and yank it to a standstill. Gee, how could anything go wrong?

So-called "broncos" and Brahma bulls are encouraged to buck by means of what are euphemistically called "flank" straps, cinched about their guts. Apologists claim the straps don't bother the beasts but it's amazing how placid they become as soon as the straps are loosened. Call me a gay vegetarian metrosexual Commie, but the whole animal-teasing premise doesn't seem all that far removed from bull-baiting, a nineteenth-century English "sport" in which packs of dogs were turned loose to tear at a tethered bull and much merriment was had by all. Not counting the bull.

Times change. About the time this year's Stampede was winding down the Spanish region of Catalonia was making history by outlawing bullfighting, an Iberian tradition that dates back to at least the time of the Romans.

Which will mean a menu change in some Spanish restaurants I

suppose. I heard a story of one American tourist who, while ordering a meal at a plush Madrid restaurant, notices a nearby diner being served a magnificently garnished dish with two giant meatballs in the centre. He asks his waiter what it is. "Cojones de toro, señor," he is told. Bulls' testicles, fresh from the local bullfighting arena and available only after a bullfight. The tourist tries to order but is told only one dish per bullfight is available. He will have to wait until the following day. The next day he arrives at the restaurant, sits down, knife and fork at the ready. The specialty dish is placed before him, but this time he notices the meatballs are tiny, almost miniscule. He complains to the waiter who shrugs and says, "Señor, you have to understand . . . sometimes the bull wins."

Can't Lose if You Don't Buy a Ticket

My old man was a crook. A miscreant. A lawbreaker. It was probably just dumb luck that saved him from being hauled off in handcuffs and tossed in a cell. Wouldn't have taken Sherlock Holmes to nail him. Pop carried the damning evidence around in his wallet, neatly folded and tucked in behind his driver's licence.

It was an Irish Sweepstakes ticket. My dad bought one every year as did umpteen thousand other Canadian hopefuls. This was back in pre-Expo days when buying or selling Irish Sweepstakes tickets was illegal. But outlawed or otherwise the Irish Sweepstakes was the only game in town, lotteries being forbidden in Canada until 1970. And truth to tell, I never heard of anybody getting busted for buying, selling or carrying an Irish Sweepstakes ticket.

My dad certainly never got caught, but he never won, either—just like 99.9 percent of the other ticket buyers. That didn't stop customers from lining up to buy them. And it didn't take government bean counters long to figure out that there was a lucrative, untapped monetary gravy train rattling by just begging to be, ah, diverted. Quebec jumped on board first with Inter Loto in 1970; the other provinces weren't far behind. Today Canada has two national lotteries and five regional lottery corporations, all of them skimming a hearty, gurgling revenue stream from the pockets of the gullible public.

Because make no mistake: lotteries are a sucker bet. No professional gambler would waste a dime on them. You're more likely to be fricasseed in a lightning strike than to strike it rich with a lottery ticket. As someone once said, lotteries are a tax on people who aren't very good at math.

The provincial lottery where I live runs the slogan, "You can't win if you don't buy a ticket." The truth is your chances are about the same whether you buy a ticket or not.

Not that those odds deter the typical lottery player. It's all too easy and beguiling to indulge in the fantasy that I'll be the one who crosschecks the Law of Probability and wins the multi-million dollar jackpot.

And if you do win the lottery? Good luck. You'll need it because that's when the chips really hit the fan.

Contrary to popular mythology it isn't glorious to become ridiculously rich overnight. It isn't glorious and it isn't healthy either. Dr. Clive Wood, director of the Happiness, Personality and Health course at Cardiff University in Wales says: "People believe that if they win the lottery they will become hugely happier, and for a while they do, but human beings have a surprising capacity to return to where they started. The problem is that once you're wealthy you become habituated to being wealthy and you want to know what the next thing is."

Which is why the founding fathers of the nation to the south of us extolled life, liberty and—not happiness, but the pursuit of happiness. It's all in the chase, folks—and buying a ticket at the 7-Eleven and scrawling a number based on your ex-husband's birthdate multiplied by his estimated IQ is not what you'd call a huge character builder.

The only happy lottery winners seem to be the ones who truly don't let the experience change them. They achieve this by giving away their newfound fortune as quickly as possible.

Winners like Mordecai, who won $8 million in a Power Ball lottery a few years ago. Mordecai had already had quite a life. As a teenager he'd survived two years in a concentration camp and escaped to Canada where he slowly regained his health, started a small business, eventually got married and raised a family. He outlived them all. When he won the lottery he was eighty-nine and living in a modest retirement home. A reporter asked him what his plans were for the $8 million. Mordecai said he'd already figured it out. One hundred thousand dollars would be divided evenly among his five friends. The rest would go to his favourite charity, Save the Children. "Except," he said, "for one dollar. One dollar I'm giving to the Canadian Nazi Party."

The reporter was dumbfounded. The Nazis had starved and tortured him and exterminated his brothers and sisters. How, after all they had done to Mordecai and his people, could he think of giving even a dollar to the Nazis?

Mordecai shrugged, as he rolled up his right sleeve. "It's only fair," he said, pointing to his forearm. "They gave me the winning numbers."

Don't Feed the Coyotes

Graze vt. 1. to feed on (growing grass, herbage, etc.)
—COLLINS CONCISE DICTIONARY

Once upon a time in a city far away where I put in a tour of duty as a lowly city hall reporter, I encountered a magnificent specimen of the Grazing Mammal, subspecies *Homo sapiens*.

She was a city councillor, famous for her large hats, larger purses and unfailing attendance at all civic functions that featured a complimentary food bar. This city councillor would sweep in, usually about the time the function was winding down, engage in a little political banter for a few minutes and when (she thought) no one was looking, surreptitiously fill her capacious purse with canapés, pastries, celery sticks, cocktail wieners and other assorted hors d'oeuvres that were lying about.

Hey—no finger pointing here. I'm an old-time bottom feeder myself. When I was working my way through (okay, halfway through) college I had a night job as a bartender. The pay wasn't great but I survived for at least three semesters on a diet that consisted pretty much of olives, orange and lime slices, maraschino cherries and beer nuts.

On-the-job grazing kept me alive but I bear the scars. I still can't look at a pimento without gagging.

But I was strictly an amateur in the grazing field. I have a friend who worked security for a large Toronto hotel for many years. I once asked him what his biggest headache was—towel thieves? Mini-bar raiders? Drunks? Pickpockets? Peeping Toms? He shook his head.

"Convention Coyotes," he told me.

These were people—mostly men—who haunted the ballrooms and

showrooms of the larger downtown hotels. "They'd wear a suit and tie, slap on a big smile and a name tag and slip into the convention rooms around lunch time," my buddy recalled. "A lot of conventions have three, four hundred delegates in attendance, so it wasn't hard for these guys to blend right in. Some of those freeloaders ate free lunches for years."

Serious grazing takes serious nerve—but you'd have to go some to out-nerve the Kiwi who got outed in Wellington, New Zealand, recently.

At the Harbour City Funeral Home.

That's right—the guy was a fake mourner. According to funeral director Danny Langstraat the grazing griever hit at least four funerals a week, hoovering up the finger food even though he had no idea who had died.

"Certainly he had a backpack with some Tupperware containers," said Langstraat. "So when people weren't looking, he was stocking up."

Officials eventually got wise to his antics, took a photo of him in mid-forage and distributed it to all the local funeral homes. The "grim eater" was out of business.

The biggest mistake professional grazers make? Underestimating the enemy.

Like the smart aleck yuppie who cruises up to a lonely shepherd tending his flock on a hillside one afternoon, casts a smirking glance at the host of nibbling sheep and says to the shepherd, "I'm looking for a lamb dinner. If I tell you exactly how many sheep you have in your flock, will you give me one?"

The shepherd figures there's no way the yuppie can count every critter, so he nods. Instantly the yuppie whips out an iPhone, Googles a NASA app, calls up a GPS navigation system that scans his geographical location and gives him an ultra-high resolution photo of the hillside. He forwards the data to an image processing facility in Silicon Valley. Within seconds, his portable printer is delivering a four-colour, twenty-page digitized report. The yuppie glances at the report summary turns to the shepherd and says, "You have exactly six-hundred and seventy-three sheep. I'll take that lamb over there." He picks it up and places it in his car trunk.

The shepherd says, "If I tell you what your profession is, will you give me back my animal?" The yuppie snorts, says, "Sure, why not?"

"You're a business consultant," says the shepherd. The yuppie is floored. "How could you possibly know that?" he says.

"Pretty easy," says the shepherd. "You showed up here, even though nobody called you. You expect to get paid for an answer I already knew to a question I never asked—and most important: you don't know anything about my business.

"Now open your trunk and give me back my border collie."

Exercise? Easy Does It

I don't work out. If God had wanted us to bend over he'd have put diamonds on the floor.

—Joan Rivers

I'm with the Empress of Botox on this one. I find the concept of voluntary perspiration dubious. I hail from Scottish peasant stock, meaning my ancestors spent a depressing number of centuries chasing sheep through glen and over brae, waiting for the Industrial Revolution. When it arrived the upwardly mobile members of my clan graduated to twelve-hour days of semi-slavery at the mill for starvation wages. Despite the lack of health benefits or pension plan they reckoned things were looking up. Now they had a roof.

Also the Industrial Revolution was chugging along. Soon we had machines to do onerous, exhausting chores like sheep wrestling, wool plucking and heavy labour in general. Before long there were machines for pretty well everything and nobody had to lift a finger.

Then somebody noticed our fingers were getting fat. So we invented more machines—treadmills, stationary bicycles, NordicTracks, elliptical trainers, rowing machines. Now we could join health clubs and pay for the privilege of sweating like our peasant forebears.

Not my cup of tea, I'm afraid. Vigorous exercise and I have been uneasy partners ever since the time I borrowed hockey skates to play in a father–son game. The kids were adolescents; I was in my forties but miraculously my long-dormant hockey skills bloomed again. I knew which end of the stick to hold, I remembered not to shoot at our team's goalie, I even had, late in the game, an end-to-end breakaway. As I bore down on the opponents' net just ahead of the pursuing twelve-year-olds I thought, it's all coming back! My stickhandling, my crisp, rhythmic strides—everything!

Except—how to stop.

The goalie scrambled out of my way; the puck dribbled wide. I ended up like a giant, bagged grouse bulging out the back of the net.

I was equally unlucky at other athletic pursuits. I still hold the record at the Circle M dude ranch for most buck-offs by a trail horse (twelve times in twenty-five minutes). Then there was my trampoline trauma. It was an old-style trampoline, made of interlocking mesh strands instead of solid canvas. Shirtless, I soared into a front drop, landing flawlessly, swanlike even, on my chest and belly. Unfortunately, two strands of mesh elected to interlock around my left nipple. Most of my body rebounded up and away from the trampoline with the exception of my nipple, which remained securely fastened to it.

The pain was in Technicolor.

I trampole no longer. Neither do I equester, gymnase, fall down mountains while strapped to lumber or try to impersonate Sydney Crosby on sheets of ice. I follow religiously the exercise regimen devised by the late comedian Jackie Gleason.

"When I wake up each morning," said Mister G., "I always do my exercises. I tell myself sternly, 'Ready now. Up—down—up—down.' After three strenuous minutes of this, I do the same thing with my other eyelid."

First Turn Off, Then Turn In

*I have left orders to be awakened at any time in case of
national emergency. Even if I'm in a cabinet meeting.*
—RONALD REAGAN

You get enough sleep last night? Chances are you didn't. One out of
every seven Canadian adults—that's 3.3 million of us—has trouble
nodding off or staying unconscious after lights out.

It's even grimmer in the States. More than 40 percent of Americans
wake up every day feeling grumpy and sleep deprived—and the experts
at the US National Sleep Foundation think they know why. A study conducted by the foundation revealed that 95 percent of the people polled
had used some sort of electronic device less than an hour before bed.
They're not talking about radios or stereos or even electric toothbrush-
es. They're zeroing in on light-emitting gizmos like TVs, smart phones,
computers and video game players—devices a foundation spokesman
claims "can suppress the sleep-promoting hormone melatonin" and
leave us staring goggled-eyed at the ceiling, all psyched up with nowhere
to go. End result: a crummy sleep followed by a sub-standard day.

The consequences are grim too. According to the US Center for
Disease Control, "driver fatigue" causes upwards of 100,000 vehicle
crashes and 1,550 deaths in the US every year.

I spent a few months as a couch surfer during my wayward youth.
One of the places I crashed at (but never for long) belonged to a couple
who owned three TVs and ran them pretty well twenty-four hours a day.
One of the sets was in their bedroom and it stayed on all night. I could
see the grey-blue light leaking out under their bedroom door and hear

the murmur of fitness shows, get-rich-quick ads and on-air diet gurus droning through the early morning hours. One evening I got brave and asked them how come they left their bedroom TV on all night.

"Can't sleep," they said in unison.

It was a Homer Simpson moment but I let it pass.

It was also a valuable learning experience. Aside from a clock with a luminous dial sitting on a dresser against the far wall, our bedroom is a technology-free zone. True, there's a bedside telephone but through some mysterious and totally wonderful Ma Bell quirk the ringer—on that phone only—never sounds. We can phone out but we can't hear anyone trying to reach us. If you phone me after I've hit the sack you'll get a recording asking you to leave a message at the tone.

And why not? How is it that we have come to give these gadgets such control over our lives? How come so many people are incapable of having lunch in a restaurant, sitting on a park bench or relaxing to enjoy a bus ride without first checking in with their BlackBerry or iPod to see if it's okay for them to take a break?

I'm reminded of the story of Edgar Degas, the French painter and sculptor. Degas, a practising curmudgeon, had a friend named Jean-Louis Forain who loved new technology. Forain was one of the first citizens to have a telephone installed in his home in Paris. Hoping to impress Degas he invited him over for dinner, having arranged to have a friend phone the house while they were eating. They were halfway through the first course when the phone rang. Monsieur Forain leapt up to answer it. When he returned to the table smugly beaming, Degas looked up from his plate and grumbled: "So that is the telephone. It rings, and you run."

To paraphrase another well-known Francophone, Ma Bell has no place in the bedrooms of the nation. Neither does Sony, Apple, Hewlett-Packard or RCA. If you're looking for a reasonably priced, non-electronic device that you can turn to at bedtime that won't interfere with sleep I can recommend just the thing. It's a database recording system, but it's non-light-emitting, involves no dials or switches, takes no batteries and never needs recharging. Nevertheless five minutes before bedtime with this baby and you'll be out like a light—guaranteed.

It's a book called *The Collected Speeches of Stephen Harper*.

Internet: You Get What You Pay For

Spending an evening on the World Wide Web is much like
sitting down to a dinner of Cheetos . . . two hours later
your fingers are yellow and you're no longer hungry, but
you haven't been nourished.

—CLIFFORD STOLL

Hey, did you see Jimmy Kimmel get bitten by that rattlesnake? Unbelievable! Happened live on his late night TV show! Two zoo guys brought out this huge rattler supposedly restrained by a neck clamp but it broke loose, lashed out and bit Kimmel right on the hand! Happened on prime time TV. You can check it out yourself on YouTube.

On second thought, don't bother—it's a crock. Never happened— or rather it seemed to, but it was faked. It was all part of a razzle-dazzle setup to introduce Kimmel's guests that night—some of the actors who appear on the TV show *House*.

I only mention it because at least five people have emailed me the original YouTube video. All of them fervently believe it actually happened.

Hey, I was sucked in too. I only got suspicious when there was no mention of the incident in the next day's newspapers. Surely a TV show host getting fanged by a rattlesnake on prime time TV would make the front page?

It surely would. And that's my problem with the Internet. The very thing that's trumpeted as the beauty of the beast is its major problem— nobody's in charge. Everything that appears on the Internet has the weight of a lead story in the *Globe and Mail* about regime change in Ottawa.

Or a *National Enquirer* exclusive about Martians snatching Obama and replacing him with a robot.

How can you tell if what comes out of your laptop is legit? You can't, for sure. Newspapers have grumpy and suspicious editors, not to mention reporters with "news sense" and a resistance to being conned by fraudsters. The Internet, by contrast, is peppered with pimply geeks with perverted tastes and twenty-four-hour access to online photograph manipulation programs such as Photoshop. They get their kicks by gulling the gullible and they answer to no one.

A few years ago the world was stunned when a tsunami swept shorelines along the Indian Ocean killing tens of thousands. Soon after, horrific photos appeared on the Internet, including one iconic shot taken from the window of a high-rise in Phuket, Thailand. It shows a massive foaming wave sweeping across a coastal highway and about to crash into the downtown area. The photo is chilling, horrific, stupendous. And a complete fraud.

The skyline it depicts bears no resemblance to the actual skyline of Phuket. The wave that's crashing ashore is right out of *Avatar* special effects. It would appear to be at least twenty storeys high. The waves that devastated the Asian coastline were powerful but not one of them was more than twenty feet in height. Whoever put up the photo even got the highway traffic flow wrong. Thais drive on the left-hand side of the road, not the right.

An expert who analyzed the photograph determined that it actually shows the skyline of the city of Antofagasta, Chile. Different ocean, different continent.

As for the killer wave supposedly poised to strike . . . can we say "Photoshop"?

The World Wide Web is awash with bogus news stories shored up by fake photographs. Have you seen the 800-pound razorback hog shot by a hunter in Arkansas? The giant human skeleton found in the Arabian Desert? The catfish with a basketball stuck in its mouth? The carcass of the mermaid that washed ashore on a beach in South Africa?

Or in the Philippines. Or at Fort Desoto Beach in Florida, depending on what the faker who posted the video has been smoking.

A guy by the name of Rich Wurman figured out that a weekday edition of the *New York Times* contains more information than the average person was likely to come across in a lifetime in seventeenth-century England. We're in the twenty-first century now—when a school kid has access to more information in her handheld iPod than she'd find in a year's worth of *New York Times*. The difference is, most (well, much) of the crap has been edited out of the newspaper.

The scary fact is, newspapers are an endangered species; the Internet is thriving.

There is one thing you can do for yourself—put www.snopes.com in your "favourites" file. It's a website devoted to exposing frauds, rumours, myths and outright lies. If you come across a story that sets your BS antennae waving, check it out at Snopes.

Oh yeah—and keep buying newspapers. We need them more than ever.

Mama Don't Take My Kodachrome Away

A photograph is neither seized nor taken by force. It offers itself up. It is the photo that takes you.

—Henri Cartier-Bresson

There is a photograph of a busy street in France in 1838 or maybe 1839 taken by a Frenchman named Louis Daguerre. If you squint you can just make out, down in the left-hand corner, the blurry image of a man getting his boots shined.

It is the first photograph in history to show a human being.

How uncluttered—or at least un-chronicled in images—our lives must have been before that first camera shutter clicked. Today we are besieged by photographs of people. Billboards, television, movies, magazines, newspapers, tweets. Most of the images that worm their way into our consciousness are fleeting and inconsequential but every so often one snapshot has the power to seize our attention and burn into our brains.

Like the one of the Afghan girl.

That photograph burst upon the world from the cover of the July 1985 issue of *National Geographic* magazine. It showed the face, smudged and feral, of a gaunt and haunting adolescent, a ragged red scarf draped over her head, two huge eyes like emerald lasers blazing back at the lens. Her story line was as bleak as her gaze. She was an anonymous Afghan orphan living in a refugee camp. Weeks earlier Russian helicopter gunships had screamed in low, obliterating her village and machine-gunning her parents and most of her neighbours. She had fled with her siblings over the mountains to a camp in Pakistan.

And somehow all of that—and more—was in the photograph. You could see it in those eyes. The picture was irresistible and unforgettable. It went viral and eventually *National Geographic* declared it "the most recognized photograph" in the 122-year history of the magazine.

The photo was the work of Steve McCurry, an American freelance photographer, who captured it in a refugee camp in Peshawar, Pakistan. And it was taken on good old Kodachrome—the film Paul Simon sang about.

The refrain of that song goes, "Mama don't take my Kodachrome away." Well, mama had nothing to do with it but Kodachrome is gone. Kodak, opting to put all its eggs in the digital basket, discontinued the manufacture of its famous product in 2009, with one final 20,000-roll production run.

Then an amazing thing happened.

Steve McCurry, who'd spent his career and made his name shooting with Kodachrome film, contacted Kodak and asked if he could have the very last roll off the production line. Kodak executives gave McCurry the final thirty-six-exposure strip. He proceeded to plan a photo shoot as if he had the last roll of film in the world—which in a sense, he did.

He spent six weeks circling the globe looking for perfect subjects. He took a photo of Ribari tribesmen in Rajasthan and another of Bollywood stars in Mumbai. He took a shot of Grand Central Station, of the Brooklyn Bridge—and one of a taxicab, the paint job of which exactly matched that familiar, world-famous Kodachrome yellow. McCurry shot his last three frames in the small town of Parsons, Kansas, which happens to be the home of the last photo lab in the world to process Kodachrome film.

McCurry did not include a recent photo of the Afghan girl who made him famous. He'd already tracked her down back in 2002 after a seventeen-year search. McCurry discovered that her name was Sharbat Gula. She was no longer a girl but a woman, lined and weary-looking, living in a remote Afghan village with her husband and three daughters. She lives in accordance with the dictates of purdah, meaning she could not be seen by men without permission of the males in her family. They allowed her to be photographed by a female associate producer on McCurry's staff. Those famous eyes are noticeably dimmer, having perhaps seen too much.

On the bright side, her original iconic photograph has come to symbolize the suffering of an entire generation of Afghan women and children, and moved the National Geographic Society to establish the Afghan Girls Fund, which channels money and resources to educational programs in Afghanistan.

Sharbat Gula had no idea she was famous. She had never seen or even heard about the photograph known around the world.

No Head for Figures

If memory serves, I spent just one high school year studying the subject of geometry. One period a day, five days a week, forty minutes per period. The experience was nauseating, terrifying and bewildering. I can honestly say that I hated Every Single Second.

And here is the sum total of what I remember from that year of study: In a right-angled triangle, the square of the hypotenuse is equal to the sum of the squares of the other two sides.

Now ask me how many times in the decades since I have needed to know anything at all about squares on triangles. Or hypotenuses. I think this is probably the first time I have ever used the word "hypotenuse" since those dreary, dreadful days of geometry class.

I also have, in the dustbin that passes for my mind, vague memories of things called sines and cosines, logarithms and quadratic equations. Today I wouldn't know a quadratic equation from a quadriplegic Klingon. Nevertheless, I was doomed to spend uncountable hours in geometry, algebra, trigonometry and calculus classes having higher mathematical esoterica drilled into my skull.

Well, not so much "drilled into" as "ricocheted off." It seems I am genetically impervious to the joys of mathematics. All those propositions and equations pinged off my brainpan like BBs off a tin roof. Trying to teach me higher math was a colossal waste of time— both the teachers' and mine. The difference was, the teachers were getting paid.

Aside from the misery there have been two long-term detrimental effects for me. Number one, I have always felt guilty about my arithmetical impotence. Number two, I rear and freak like a spooked horse at the mere sight of numbers I'm expected to do something with. Figure out my bank balance? GAAAAH! Calculate my height in centimetres? Mercy! Decide which coat to choose when the weather forecast says "twenty-kilometre winds and a high of plus seven"? I give up—wear a parka and prepare to sweat.

I'm not belittling mathematics per se. The writer Don De Lillo defines mathematics as "what the world is when we subtract our own perceptions" and I'm okay with that. I'm also aware that one of the great scientific treatises of the renaissance was a book called *Ars Magna* (The Great Art). It was subtitled *The Rules of Algebra*. Fine. No argument. I'm just saying that mathematics and me equals the Date from Hell.

Turns out I can finally let the guilt go. An item in a recent issue of the *New York Times* says that algebra, trig and calculus instruction is wasted on students who have no aptitude for higher math—indeed, on anyone not heading for a career in engineering or science.

What makes the article compelling is the fact that the two authors, Sol Garfunkel and David Mumford, are career mathematicians, which is to say they know their *Ars Magna* from a hole in the ground.

They make the argument that society would be much better served if math duds like me were given a course in what they call "quantitative literacy," which is to say, we should have been taught the basics of handling our own finances, plus relatively straightforward concepts such as percentages, probability and risk.

In other words, mathematics that could actually be useful as opposed to, say, squares on the hypotenuses of right-angled triangles.

Makes sense to me. Last year, a spokeswoman for the Vanier Institute of the Family announced that when you factor in mortgages, credit cards debt and lines of credit, the average Canadian family is carrying $100,000 in debt. Perhaps with a better grounding in basic math more folks would figure out that maxing out their Visa or American Express and paying a Mafia-worthy interest rate of 20 percent on the balance is actually kind of a crummy deal. You don't have to be Albert Einstein to get that.

Speaking of whom, can you explain what the most famous equation of all time—$E=mc^2$—actually means?

Me neither. But don't feel bad. Somebody once said, "Since the mathematicians have attacked the Relativity Theory, I myself no longer understand it."

The somebody who said that was Albert Einstein.

Plainly Because of the Meat

I have no doubt that it is a part of the destiny of the human race, in its gradual improvement, to leave off eating animals, as surely as the savage tribes have left off eating each other when they came in contact with the more civilized.

—HENRY DAVID THOREAU, WALDEN

For what it's worth, the duck never knew what hit him. A blue-winged teal beating his way south along a chain of lakes and rivers in Muskoka country. I was a fifteen-year-old kid shivering behind a log on the riverbank. I picked up the whistle of his wings first, thumbed the safety off my Remington, saw him barrelling toward me, five feet off the water. I drew a bead, aimed ahead of him by a few feet as I'd been taught, and when he was abreast of me, I pulled the trigger. The duck cartwheeled in a puff of feathers and hit the water like a kid doing a cannonball. My ears ached. There was massive silence. The duck—a carcass now—bobbed peacefully on the surface of the water.

It was a momentary thrill soon overlapped by a greater sadness. I felt like I'd farted in a cathedral—disturbed and distorted a larger narrative than mine. I had a good breakfast in my belly and a hearty lunch awaited me back at the cottage. I didn't need duck meat.

But I retrieved the carcass, plucked and cleaned it and that night I ate it, gingerly spitting out pickles of buckshot from time to time. It's the only meat I ever ate that I killed myself.

The experience did not turn me into a vegetarian, rather, a

hypocritical carnivore. I continued to eat meat; I just let others do the actual dirty work.

And I knew better than most how dirty that work was. My father was a livestock salesman. He bought sheep and calves at the Ontario Public Stock Yards and I worked beside him for several summers. We were middlemen on the commercial food chain. We bought live animals trucked in by farmers and sold them in job lots to buyers from Canada Packers, the slaughterhouse across the street. Technically we had no blood on our boots but we were enablers up to our eyeballs.

Well, all of this preamble to explain my ongoing uneasy relationship with meat and the way we get it to our plates. Have I tried vegetarianism? Yes—for the best part of three years once. But a man can eat only so many spinach casseroles. The truth is I still salivate over sirloin, jockey for first dibs on a turkey drumstick and believe the aroma of frying bacon to be right up there with the smell from a freshly opened tin of Erinmore Flake pipe tobacco.

So. A hearty carnivore and un-proud of it. Is there any salvation for this mindless sinner?

Maybe. It's called IVM, which stands for in-vitro meat. It is, to be simplistic, meat that's grown in a test tube—no fat, no bone, no organs or gristle—also no swine flu, avian flu, mad cow or brucellosis. No sentient life, in fact.

Is it unnatural? Hell, yes. IVM is eight kinds of blasphemy, guaranteed to outrage everybody from Glen Beck to Martha Stewart. IVM will have cattle farmers, pork producers, sheep ranchers and poultrymen (not to mention all the fishermen at sea) looking for new lines of work. Slaughterhouses will be transformed into trendy condos; grazing lands (70 percent of the world's arable land is currently devoted to livestock) will be freed up for other crops, real estate or—more blasphemy— return to its natural state.

People will never eat lab meat you say? Check the pedigree of the stuff that's being peddled down at the supermarket right now. Some of those sanitized gobbets of pink flesh in shrink-wrapped plastic film are so laced with steroids, growth hormones and antibiotics it's a wonder they don't glow in the dark.

So what about IVM—will it fly? Don't ask me, I'm a scribbler, not a soothsayer. But I do believe if we all got to walk through a slaughterhouse on a business day 95 percent of us would exit the building as vegetarians.

I'll say this too: If in-vitro meats do replace slaughtered animals it will be as transformative for humans as the invention of the wheel or the discovery of steam.

I'll say one other thing: "My will contains directions for my funeral, which will be followed not by mourning coaches, but by oxen, sheep, flocks of poultry, and a small travelling aquarium of live fish, all wearing white scarves in honour of the man who perished rather than eat his fellow creatures."

Actually, I didn't say that. George Bernard Shaw did.

Read Any Good Emails Lately?

Had a couple visiting us from Washington last week.

Make that half a couple. The guy was charming, witty, interesting and eager to explore new places.

His wife was wired.

Almost literally. She's an investment something-or-other back in Washington and I don't know why she wasted money on the trip because she never really left her office. First day she plunked her laptop on the dining room table, flipped it open, turned it on . . . and seldom took her eyes off it for the next three days. She was constantly "following the market" or "wrangling emails" or "checking eBay." When she did manage to break free of the laptop's hypnotic tractor beam she still wasn't really in the room with us. Her eyes would wander and before long she'd lurch spasmodically, haul her BlackBerry out of her pocket and smile apologetically. "Getting an email," she would murmur. Then she would turn away from the table to peck out her response.

She wasn't being intentionally rude; she couldn't help herself. There's a viral contagion sweeping the globe and she's got it bad. I wish Marshall McLuhan was still around—he'd encapsulate what's going on in one gnomic epigram. What it looks like to me is we are, all of us, being wired into one continuous, unblinking, earth-encircling electric circuit.

Consider this: In 1815 it took weeks for news of the outcome of the Battle of Waterloo to reach the ears of the citizens of Edinburgh. Last year anyone with a smart phone anywhere in the world could track the London riots in real time.

Or consider this: A recent Angus Reid poll found that one out of five Canadians—20 percent of us—would turn down a million dollars rather than lose our Internet access.

When I read that in the paper I found it so unbelievable I had to check it. Seems like it's true. In the online poll 1,009 Canadians were asked the following question: "Would you rather receive one million dollars and never use the Internet again or would you prefer to keep the Internet?" Yup, you guessed it: 20 percent of the respondents said they'd rather be online than be a millionaire.

You don't have to be a tech junkie to be affected by the seductive siren call of the Internet. I don't do Facebook or Twitter (does anyone aside from hospital patients in full body casts truly have time for that?) but I get way more emails than I need in my life—and I spend way too many hours dealing with them.

There are only twenty-four hours in the day and if we're spending more and more time online it means we're spending less and less time doing something else. For some people it means less sleep; others lose out on sports and recreational activities.

For me, it's books. I am not reading nearly as many books as I used to.

I want to. I still buy books and start them. Then they join the teetering stacks of unread or half-read tomes beside my bed. I just can't concentrate as well as I used to. I can no longer, as literary critic David Ulin wrote, "find within myself the quiet necessary to read." I think it's because I'm subconsciously waiting for the book to beep or ping or buzz or transport me to a related video link. I think I'm actually waiting for—expecting—a distraction that will titillate me, divert me, take me away from the grunt work of reading.

Oh, I still ingest reams of data—blogs, YouTube videos, favourite websites and clever stuff my friends send me. Trouble is, it's mostly crap or at best entertaining minutiae that won't mean a thing two months from now. A good book is a three-course meal; an hour on the Internet is like ODing on granddad's BBQ pork rinds.

A good book is the opposite of that. It's the distillation of a premise or an idea or a flight of fancy that someone thought was worthy of preserving in a form that wouldn't change for centuries. As Samuel Butler said, "The oldest books are just out to those who haven't read them."

Don't mistake me—I'm not dissing the Internet. It's revolutionary and it's mind-blowing. Internet technology is the biggest thing to come along in my lifetime—so far.

But when it comes to content, I'm not sure about the shelf life.

Stop the World, I Wanna Get Off

I sometimes wonder if our planet is the asylum of the universe for disordered minds.

—GOETHE

Ever get the feeling you've been shanghaied into showing up at the wrong cocktail party? Or perhaps downloaded onto the wrong planet?

It's the little jarring signs, such as finding yourself living next to a nation that is in the process of selecting candidates for Supreme Leader—and the contenders are as bizarre a collection of nutbars, fruit-cakes, Flat Earthers and tin pot fascists as you could find this side of the bar scene in *Star Wars*.

Or hearing the news that baseball fans lined up to pay $250 a pop for a half-ounce of clay taken from the baseball diamond where Derek Jeter got his three-thousandth major league hit last summer. Other mementoes from that game available for purchase: thirty baseballs used during the game ($2,000 each); first, second and third base ($7,500 per bag); and one pair of Jeter's sweaty socks ($1,000—all prices USD, no HST).

How about the results of that survey recently conducted by London's Museum of Science? It asked 3,000 Britons to list things they absolutely could not live without.

According to science the correct answers are: air, water, food, sleep and sex. According to the British survey results air, sleep and sex don't even make the top ten. Four absolute indispensables that do: the mobile phone, Internet connection, email and Facebook.

No wonder increasing numbers of citizens can be seen jaywalking down the streets staring off into space and jabbering to themselves like lunatics.

Oh, sorry. Those are Bluetooth customers.

First time I saw a guy decked out in a Bluetooth earpiece in a restaurant I thought I was witnessing the victim of a hideously botched plastic surgery experiment. The gizmo gives off a whiff of robot and always struck me as the ultimate in über-geekdom, but hey, I've still got vinyl records so what do I know?

Speaking of whiffs, are you familiar with the work of Christopher Brosius? No?

Where have you been, child? Christopher Brosius is a New York *parfumier*—he manufactures perfumes. Some people—especially Christopher Brosius—think that he's quite possibly the most talented and innovative perfume maker in the world.

He's come up with some doozies, alright. Brosius specializes in fragrances that invoke memories of childhood—hence his offering of phials and atomizers that dispense scents of Green Bean, Baseball Glove and (my favourite) Clean Baby Butt.

But that's minor league stuff for Christopher Brosius. Like a psychic bloodhound he's got his nose high in the air sniffing the next perfume frontier. A perfume so subtle, so evanescent, so exclusive . . .

. . . that no one will be able to smell it.

He's already got a name for the wonder fragrance. He's going to call it Where We Are There Is No Here.

Perfect. Especially for a perfume maker with a website called "I Hate Perfume."

I think I might have managed to hang on to my few remaining marbles had I not come across another news story. DYLAN TAKING UP THE PIPES, the headline reads.

Oh, please, god—no. Bob Dylan and the Scottish bagpipes??? The Marquis de Sade couldn't have thought that up.

As a man with an impeccable Scottish pedigree (Clan MacGregor) and a mouldy collection of Bob Dylan's first LPs, let me declare my bias right up front: I think Dylan wrote some of the best popular music of the twentieth century—but he hasn't uttered an intelligible lyric in the past thirty years. Theoretically that makes him a good match for the bagpipes, which when played properly still sound like a hyena being water boarded.

And yet Dylan travels the world constantly, playing sold-out concert after sold-out concert, during each of which he comes on stage, ignores the audience, mumbles and growls through a medley of his hits in the wrong key, singing the wrong words, playing in the wrong tempo . . . and leaves the stage to a standing ovation. Pretty soon he'll be doing all that—and playing the bagpipes.

A French philosopher by the name of Augustus Saint-Gaudens once said: "What garlic is to a salad, insanity is to art."

Perhaps some day Dylan will write a song about that.

Not that we'll ever understand him when he sings it.

Steve Jobs, What Have You Done?

One sunny Saturday when I was a little kid my big sister took me to the beach. She picked up a seashell and put it next to my ear. "Listen," she said. "You can hear the ocean."

Damned if I couldn't. I thought it was a miracle. I took that shell home and put it on my dresser. Every once in a while I'd pick it up and listen to the faraway ocean waves.

My first long-distance call.

It was good practice for the telephone on our kitchen wall that was the next thing I held at my ear and listened to. I couldn't hear waves but if I breathed through my nose and remembered not to cough I could listen to old Mrs. Paton gossip with old Mrs. Chapman (we had a rural party line).

My next technological lurch forward was the pay telephone—specifically the pay phone in the hallway of a flophouse I lived in for a summer in Montreal. Leo, the saxophone-noodling, pot-smoking landlord, had a bent piece of coat hanger dangling from a string attached to the phone. When you stuck the wire into the coin return slot and twisted it just so you had free long distance. Feed a coin into the phone and it registered as a deposit, but came right back to you through the return slot. You just fed it back into the phone as many times as necessary.

Using a pay phone was never easier. Certainly not in Britain, where you dialled your number and got connected, whereupon a tony robot voice asked you to "Please deposit sixpence." By the time you did, the party you were calling had often hung up.

That was still better than Spain, where you couldn't even use a pay phone until you found someone willing to sell you a *ficha*—a metal slug with a hole in the middle of it. That was the only "coin" Spanish pay phones would accept.

I was nudged into this telephonic reverie by something I saw during the World Series: team manager Tony La Russa in the St. Louis Cardinals dugout, yakking away . . . on a pay phone. They still use them in big league baseball dugouts.

Which is heart-warming, because the North America pay telephone is the ivory-billed woodpecker of communications technology—so endangered it might as well be extinct.

You used to find them everywhere—corner stores, gas stations, laundromats, hotel lobbies, hospital waiting rooms, even on roadsides. Now outside pay phones are rarer than Sasquatch sightings. Mobile phones did that. In Europe there are more cellphones than there are people. Here in Canada cellphone usage is nudging 80 percent of the market. Many of the outside public phones that still exist are regularly ravaged by meth heads looking for change. The phone companies won't be replacing those feverishly—if ever.

It's a trend that's unlikely to be reversed. People used to appreciate the convenience of a public telephone but I doubt anyone ever fell in love with them—not like cellphones.

And love is not too strong a word to use—particularly for the unseemly bond that unites many iPhone owners with their devices. An American branding consultant by the name of Martin Lindstrom recently conducted an experiment in which he studied the brain wave patterns of sixteen subjects interacting with their iPhones.

According to Lindstrom, when the subjects heard or saw their iPhones, the insular cortex of their brains showed the same activity that is associated with love. Yup, these people were actually in love with their iPhones.

I don't get it. But then, I'm a geezer. I remember when wise guys answered the phone saying, "Your dime; my time"—because that's what it cost to make a call from a pay phone way back then. You didn't need a fifty-dollar-a-month contract and a pricey piece of plastic in your pocket. All you needed was a pay phone and a ten-cent piece. For that you'd even get the assistance of a helpful, actually human operator to flirt with as she walked you through the call.

I wonder what happened to all those wonderful operators. I

know there are jobs out there waiting if they want them. Why, Aegis Communications Limited just put out a call for 10,000 employees to work in their nine new call centres fielding customer-service problems.

Aegis is an Indian corporation based in Mumbai but that doesn't mean anyone has to move. The company plans to outsource those 10,000 jobs to the US to take advantage of cheap labour.

Hey, you know those Americans. They'll work almost for nothing.

Too Much Information!

For a list of all the ways technology has failed to improve the quality of life, press three.

—ALICE KAHN

I have a simple relationship with my telephone: I talk to it; it talks to me. Not conversationally, you understand. More like ships passing in the night, or two drunks raving in a bar. Here, for instance, is a transcript of the conversation that ensued when I asked my Telephone Person about my old messages:

TELEPHONE PERSON: "PLEASE ENTER YOUR PASSWORD, FOLLOWED BY THE POUND SIGN."

ME: PUNCHPUNCHPUNCHPUNCH . . . POUND

TP: "YOU HAVE NO NEW MESSAGES AND FIVE OLD MESSAGES. TO LISTEN TO YOUR OLD MESSAGES, PRESS SIX."

ME: PUNCH

TP: "YOU ARE REVIEWING OLD MESSAGES." (I knew that). "TO LISTEN TO YOUR OLD MESSAGES, PRESS ONE."

ME: PUNCH!

TP: "PLAYING OLD MESSAGES."

Now does that seem unnecessarily dopey and circuitous or am I just being crotchety? I remember, coot that I am, when to retrieve messages I just dialled zero and said, "Hi, Alice . . . any messages?" "Yes," she would say. "A bill collector and your mother-in-law. I told them you were in a meeting."

I miss Alice.

I miss all the receptionists, secretaries, operators, stenos, temps and other human beings who have been vaporized and replaced by the Telephone Person who pretends to be human but is really just a recording and wouldn't know my mother-in-law from Lady Gaga. Or me from you, come to that. I liked it better before the ethereal robots from Planet Call Waiting took over.

Take elevators. Used to be if I found myself in a high-rise lobby with a wish to go to the twelfth floor I would get in the elevator and press twelve. After a decent interval the door would slide open and hey, presto! I would be on the twelfth floor, just as I'd planned.

Not anymore. Now an elevator trip is an excursion—complete with an electronic cheerleader. The elevator beeps at every floor as I ascend and a disembodied voice that sounds like Darth Vader with sinusitis does the math for me. BEEP! "SEG–GUND FLOOR" BEEP! "THIRD FLOOR . . ." There is no real need for me to know the precise moment I am passing floors two through eleven because: (a) I memorized that arithmetic sequence back in kindergarten; and (b) I'm not stopping at any of those floors—and hopefully, the elevator isn't either. If I'm wrong about that, I'll know right away because, er, the elevator will stop and the light will obligingly blink the floor number that interfered with my plans.

Too much information can be problematic. But don't take my word for it. Ask Search and Rescue—the folks who pluck feckless campers and trekkers out of the backcountry when they get into trouble. The advent of cellphones and portable GPS gadgets has spawned a whole new set of "emergency" situations for S&R teams to deal with.

A Rocky Mountain park spokesman told a *New York Times* reporter, "We have seen people who have solely relied on GPS technology but were not using common sense or maps or compasses."

Like the hikers who called from a mountaintop in Jackson Hole, Wyoming, requesting a guide "and some hot chocolate, please."

Or the emergency distress call from a group of hikers in the Grand Canyon last fall that resulted in a helicopter being sent out. The hikers explained to the helicopter crew that the water in their canteens "tasted salty."

Needless to say the people who risk their skins to bail out the hapless, the helpless and the hopeless are not amused when they find a gaggle of nitwit nimrods equipped with little more than a cellphone or a GPS unit. Search and Rescue sorties are not only risky, they're expensive. A typical helicopter pickup can cost $3,000.

So if you really want to test yourself against the wilderness with little more than your iPhone or your Garmin in your back pocket, go ahead. But there is one other piece of equipment you should pack.

Your cheque book.

No Nooks for Nukes

Mostly I try to use this space to amuse you folks. I like to make people smile, even chuckle on a good day. If I can find something funny in the headlines and give it a spin until it does a pratfall or a face plant, that's what I'll do.

But sometimes the news coughs up something that is so deeply unfunny it moves me to take off my jester's hat in favour of something more appropriate.

Like a haz-mat suit.

I'm thinking particularly of a front-page story written by Doug Saunders, the *Globe and Mail*'s chief European correspondent. It took up the entire front page of Saturday *Globe* last year, when Japan's Fukushima nuclear plant was approaching full meltdown. The gist of Saunders' commentary: what a shame that this catastrophe should occur *just when we need to build more nuclear plants than ever.* (Italics mine.)

I read it three times to make sure I wasn't hallucinating. Nope, that's what the man wrote. He argues that nuclear power is far cleaner and hence more beneficial for the planet than coal-fired power. And he's not alone. He quotes George Monbiot, a world-class environmental activist who is greener than the Jolly verdantly hued Giant, and who writes: "Even when nuclear power plants go horribly wrong, they do less damage to the planet and its people than coal-burning stations operating normally."

To which I can only respond: Gimme a break.

We haven't seen "horribly wrong" yet. Three-Mile Island? A hiccup. Chernobyl? A belch. Fukushima? Well, we don't know yet, but pundits are already declaring that the global alarm and arm waving was ridiculously hysterical and over the top.

Our tech boys can handle this stuff. Always have.

Of course, "always" is a relative term. Spent nuclear fuel—of which we already have 250,000 tons tucked out of sight around the planet—will remain poisonously radioactive for the next hundred thousand years. How long is that? Well, a hundred thousand years ago your relatives and mine were crouched behind boulders throwing rocks and jabbing pointed sticks at ground sloths and woolly mammoths.

But never mind a hundred thousand years or even ten thousand years, let's go back just one thousand years—one-hundredth of the lifespan of a spent fuel rod. One thousand years ago my kin were gnawing turnips, molesting sheep and dodging Vikings. That's a mere ten centuries and I'm guessing your kin weren't doing much better. With spent nuclear fuel we're talking about substances that will be fatal to all life forms for a thousand centuries.

Try to fathom for a moment the colossal arrogance of anyone—newspaper columnist, scientific spokesman or government flunky—confidently making plans to deal with containment of the deadliest of poisons that will remain toxic for the next three thousand generations of humankind.

What could go wrong in a hundred thousand years—I mean, aside from earthquakes, tsunamis, world wars, terrorist attacks, empire collapses, plagues, meteor strikes . . .

Well, there's always polar shift. There is a theory out there that from time to time the earth's crust suddenly shifts, like the skin of an apple moving around the core. It is, as I say, a theory and not a widely held one because there's no real proof. Still it would go some distance to explaining the puzzling discovery of mammoth carcasses in Siberia perfectly preserved—flash-frozen, as it were—their mouths and bellies full of grasses and buttercups never known to grow in Siberia.

National Enquirer-style hogwash? Well, somebody thought well enough of scientist Charles Hapgood's 1954 book *Earth's Shifting Crust* to write an enthusiastic foreword.

Chap named Albert Einstein.

Time is the problem. We have a planet that unfolds in epochs, politicians that think in four-year cycles and pundits who salivate to four-hour news cycles. Einstein got it. His most famous contribution boils down to three words: time is relative.

Perhaps Einstein's friend Erwin Schrodinger had the best handle on it. "Love a girl with all your heart," he advised, "and kiss her on the mouth: then time will stop and space will cease to exist."

Sure beats dodging abandoned nuclear fuel rods.

Mind you, Doug Saunders, George Monbiot and all the other nuclear power cheerleaders are absolutely right—nuclear power really is the safest, cleanest, most reliable energy source we've got.

Until it isn't.

PART FOUR

We Are All
Canuckistanis Together

Here's Toe You!

There are strange things done 'neath the midnight sun
By the men who moil for gold . . .

Indeed there are, Robert Service. I've even done a few of them myself—including (hugely unsuccessfully) moil for gold. I've also fallen off a dogsled, stuck my head down a wolf den and crossed the Yukon River on breaking ice. (These feats were accomplished in my green and rowdy youth. Alcohol, not to mention stupidity, was usually involved.)

The Arctic trails have their secret tales
That could make your blood run cold . . .

. . . such as the night I tried to sing "Allouette" in the bar at Diamond Tooth Gertie's. Or the time we ran the Chain Saw Races (don't ask) on the ice of Lake Laberge.

All of which is not to suggest I am some hardened leathery Yukoner who spent years north of sixty. Nope, I'm an outsider, a visitor, a tourist. A sourdough I am definitely not.

But sourtoe? Ah, I can speak to that.

There is this hotel, you see, in downtown Dawson called the, er, Downtown Hotel. It looks like most of the hotels and buildings in Dawson—clapboard siding, wooden floors, no frills, no neon—but it has one distinguishing feature.

The Downtown Hotel is the only drinking establishment *in the world* where you can order and drink a Sourtoe Cocktail.

A Sourtoe Cocktail is pretty straightforward. First the bartender gives you a glass full of Yukon Jack, a sweet-tasting whisky. There is no lime slice, no ice, no perky paper umbrella sticking out of it, but the Sourtoe Cocktail does contain one garnish that sets it aside from all other mixed drinks this side of the bar in *Star Wars*. At the bottom of your glass you will see something lurking that looks like a mutant peanut or a twisted hank of rope.

Except there's a nail on the end of it. A human nail. You have a severed human toe in your glass.

The origins of the Sourtoe Cocktail are lost in time. Some claim a Klondiker accidentally chopped off his toe while splitting wood one winter and never got around to throwing it away. Come spring he limped into town, ordered a beer, plopped his wizened appendage in the glass and announced "I'm gonna take a leak; nobody touch my drink while I'm gone." Nobody did. The tradition of the Sourtoe Cocktail was born.

It has evolved to this: Back of the bar in the Downtown Hotel there is a locked wooden box. Inside the box, embalmed in a jar of salt, resides the "current" Sourtoe. More about "current" later.

Your assignment, should you choose to become a member of the elite Sourtoe Club, is to: (a) pay $5 for a membership card; (b) pay $5 for your Sourtoe Cocktail; (c) drain your glass.

Wait a minute! Surely you don't have to . . .

No. But the Toe Captain will tell you: "Drink it fast or drink it slow; your lips must touch this gnarly toe."

Like most initiates I chose to drink mine fast. Like most initiates I still shudder when I remember that mummified digit bumping against my upper lip.

Some first-timers in their haste drink the cocktail a little TOO fast. That's why we have a "current" category of toes—because occasionally somebody swallows the toe and it must be replaced. Where do they find a replacement? Don't ask.

Isn't it illegal to sell drinks with human parts in them? Of course, but this is Dawson. They don't get many government inspector types up there. Besides, technically the bar doesn't "sell" you a Sourtoe Cocktail. They sell you a glass of whisky. What you choose to put in it is up to you.

What kind of idiot would choose to join the Sourtoe Club? About 65,000 of us so far. I'm not sure why, although once again I suspect that alcohol and stupidity are contributing factors. I can't even prove I belong because I misplaced my membership card years ago. And I can't reapply because I don't drink anymore.

Mind you, I still have plenty of stupid.

It's Hockey Not in Canada!

I shot it again and it went right along the ice and I saw it go in the Holy Geez.

Ah, yes. The blessed simplicity of hockey. Paul Henderson, there, trying to articulate the goal of his life—the goal of our lives—in Moscow back in 1972.

Canadian literati will tell you that we are a nation of emerging world-class writers—Munro, Atwood, Richler, Ondaatje. Minstrel meisters will hymn praises of our singers—Cohen, k.d. lang, Ben Heppner. Academics will point with pride to the deep thinkers we've produced like Northrop Frye and Marshal McLuhan. And of course sports purists can be relied upon to huff and sniff that Canada's true national sport is lacrosse, not hockey . . .

Who are they kidding? On some primeval level Canada is hockey and hockey is Canada. "The Canadian specific," poet Al Purdy called it. As undeniable when Henderson scored in Moscow as it was a thousand times when Gretzky danced along the ice or when Bobby Orr won the Stanley Cup in 1970 beating the goalie in overtime, soaring like Superman through the air, with a grin as wide as Parry Sound and his stick already raised in triumph.

And of course, Sid the Kid in Vancouver.

But you don't have to go to the Olympics or to Boston or Moscow to savour the glory of Canadian hockey. It's on the street outside our front doors from early autumn to late spring every year. You hear it in the scrape of sticks on pavement, the thwack of a slap-shot tennis ball and the yips and yelps of kids from six to fifty-six.

Road hockey. No referees, no time outs except for passing cars, minimal equipment and play goes on 'til dinner time or the light gets bad. Now THAT'S Canadian.

Or used to be. Imagine the look on the face of David Sasson when an official looking sedan with "BYLAW ENFORCEMENT" emblazoned on the door rolled up to interrupt his game of road hockey recently. Mr. Sasson is a father of a seven-year-old son and they're both hockey nuts. They live in the Montreal suburb of Dollard-des-Ormeaux and every so often the Sassons rustle up a gang of neighbourhood kids, set up some rubber boots for goal posts and play a game of road hockey out on the street in front of their place.

As they were doing when the Law showed up. The Bylaw Enforcement officers explained that they were responding to a complaint from a neighbour about "excessive noise." The game had to stop. Now.

David Sasson replied, "You're kidding—right?"

They weren't. They slapped Mr. Sasson with a $75 fine.

Turns out that it is illegal to play road hockey—not just on the backroads of Dollard-des-Ormeaux but in neighbourhoods, communities and even whole municipalities right across Canada. It's a fining offence in Port Coquitlam, BC, and Nepean, Ontario, and Rothesay, New Brunswick.

Toronto's a little sneakier about it. It's not outright illegal in Hogtown but you have to choose your venues carefully. Some streets are okay; others are forbidden. If you want to play, better bring along a lawyer.

On second thought, don't. Lawyers, as usual, are part of the problem. Some town councils and municipalities have instituted the road hockey bans to ward off possible lawsuits.

Hockey illegal in Canada? That's like banning bratwurst in Germany. Or kissing in France.

The Dollard-des-Ormeaux minions of the law picked the wrong guy to cross-check when they tried to knock Dave Sasson off the puck. First thing Dave did, he called a pal on the local newspaper. Who called several colleagues at Montreal radio and TV stations. Next, Dave organized a (sort of) impromptu road hockey game—on the street in front of the Dollard-des-Ormeaux municipal offices.

Two hundred people with hockey sticks showed up.

So far the mayor—also a hard-nose—is hanging tough. He vows

the bylaw will not be changed but the story is mushrooming beyond the control of mere politicos. Sidney Crosby has thrown in his support, there's a petition going across the country and a pro-road-hockey Facebook group has been organized out of Wilfrid Laurier University.

Don't look now, Mr. Mayor, but this game is already over.

You let in the winning goal. Slap shot through the five-hole.

Le Style—C'est l'Homme

The next few words on this page may lose me half the readership of Canada, but . . . when I think of style with a capital "S," I think of Trudeau.

Style and Trudeau go together like Toller Cranston and a triple Salchow; Oscar Peterson and a Steinway; Gretzky and a puck. Love him or loathe him (and I never met anyone who was lukewarm in their assessment) the man had style. Back in the sleepy mid-twentieth century pokey old Canada, still plaid shirted and ear muffed, had never beheld his like—certainly not among the inhabitants of 24 Sussex. We haven't yet. Can you imagine Joe Clark sliding down a banister? Paul Martin doing a pirouette? Stephen Harper wearing a cape?

Only one Canadian political figure ever tried to emulate Trudeau's public panache—Alliance leader Stockwell Day in his infamous too-sexy-for-my-wetsuit Sea-Doo press conference on a BC beach in 2000. Canadians laughed so hard he nearly drowned.

Anyone behaving like Trudeau risks being scorned as a dandified fop, but somehow the Jesuit/playboy/philosopher/politician pulled it off. A nation swooned, Trudeaumania reigned and the baying hounds of the Canadian media, recognizing a real pit bull when they saw one, assumed the downward dog yoga pose and stayed in it for the fifteen years Trudeau dominated Canadian politics. He didn't so much deal with media types as toy with them. Reporters knew they were always one fatuous question away from a withering put-down. They pretty well gave him a free pass.

It didn't hurt that the man was brilliant (Harvard, the Sorbonne, London School of Economics), adventurous (judo brown belt, white-water wilderness canoeist) and studly (moonlight skinny dipping with Liona Boyd).

He was also, as near as I can tell, fearless. In 1968 a riot broke out at the Saint-Jean-Baptiste Day parade in Montreal. Dignitaries dove for cover as cameras rolled and separatists pelted the grandstand with bottles. Not Trudeau. The prime minister refused to cower, glaring pugnaciously at the rowdies and declaring that he "would not be intimidated by a drunken mob."

I witnessed this junkyard dog side of Trudeau on a beach in rural New Brunswick of all places. Trudeau was there *en famille*, no bodyguards, barefoot and bare-chested, a picnic hamper under one arm and a toddler—Justin, I'm guessing—holding his other hand. A rough-looking guy, big, scowling, blocked his path and growled something in French. I didn't catch it but I could tell that it wasn't a marriage proposal. Trudeau put down the picnic hamper, walked up to the guy, stared into his eyes from about eight inches out and replied calmly.

Dirty Harry calmly. The would-be antagonist seemed to get smaller before my eyes. He murmured something and shuffled off.

Trudeau was not a big man—a wiry five foot nine or so—but he maintained what matadors call a serious *querencia*—an area around him that he utterly dominated. Matadors are very wary of violating a bull's *querencia*. Good advice when dealing with Trudeau as well.

A personality that big couldn't please everyone and Trudeau didn't. He was widely loathed in the Canadian west and, ironically, by tens of thousands in his home province of Quebec. Separatists called him a *vendu*—a sellout. Trudeau didn't give a damn what they called him.

He drove, famously, a 1960 Mercedes-Benz 300 SL roadster, even before he moved into 24 Sussex. A reporter asked him if he'd be giving up the Mercedes when he became PM. Trudeau replied: "Are you talking about the car now, or the girl?" Driving away, he added, "I won't give up either."

The man had style.

Newfie. Say it Loud, Say it Proud

May I politely request that from this day on everyone drop the term "Newfie"? It is as objectionable to Newfoundlanders as the other "N" word is to black people.

—Letter to the editor, January 2010

Um, with all due respect: no it's not and no I won't. I've never met a Newfoundlander who objected to the label, nor have I ever heard any outlander use the term sneeringly or hatefully. Where I come from "Newfie" is a term of endearment. As for comparison with the other "N" word, please remember that Dick Gregory, the black comedian, chose to call his best-selling autobiography *Nigger*. As he explained to his mother in the forward to the book, "Always remember, Mom, when you overhear the word 'nigger' that they're advertising my book."

And anyway, I get nervous when people start declaring which words can and can't be used. Nothing good can come of that. Words don't own us. It's the other way around.

Besides, it's too late to proscribe this particular "N" word. The term bestrides the world like a grinning, good-natured colossus. Google "newfie" and you'll be offered Newfie jokes, Newfie slang, Newfie music, Newfie songs, Newfie recipes, Newfie sayings and a Newfie dictionary.

Dig a little deeper and you will discover the Newfie Bullet, a train that ran (sporadically) between St. John's and Port aux Basques from 1898 up to the mid-1960s. The "Bullet" part of the name was a Newfie joke in itself for the train was, uh, not known for its speed. Indeed, it was prone to crawl across the province, frequently stopping for high winds, lost hunters, steep grades and jaywalking moose.

Newfie is also used to refer to the Newfoundland dog, one of the most amiable, beautiful and altogether magnificent canine breeds ever to sprinkle a fire hydrant.

And of course there's Newfie screech, a rum-based libation that can blister paint, dissolve horseshoes and cause smoke tendrils to issue from the ears of drinkers. Legend has it that screech was "distilled" from the scrapings of oaken barrels that had been used to carry both rum and molasses. After a few years a particularly potent encrustation grew on the inside of said barrels. This crust was boiled out of the barrel with hot water, cut with a few gallons of grain alcohol and served to anyone foolish enough to drink it.

Which is another Newfie joke. I never met a Newfoundlander who had much time for screech. Tourists, yes—once, anyway.

Newfie jokes? Well, I suppose if you're thin-skinned and prone to political correctness you might find Newfie jokes offensive. But the best one I ever heard came from the lips of a waiter in a bar on Duckworth Street in St. John's. He'd been serving a table of "come-from-aways" and eavesdropping on their jokes about Newfoundland. He came to their table, set down his beer tray and said:

"Feller from Tarana moved to St. John's last year. He was shaving in the bathroom one morning after he'd been here a couple of months. Looked in the mirror and saw a brown ring right across his forehead. He scrubbed at it with a washcloth but it wouldn't budge.

"So he went to the doctor and said, 'What is it, doc? Do I have a disease?' The doctor looked at him and said, 'You're not from here, are ya?'

"'No,' the feller says, 'I'm from Tarana—how could you tell?'

"Doctor says, 'Ye've got nothin' to worry about, bye—yer just fulla shit and down a quart.'"

But that's not my favourite Newfie joke. My favourite is a true story. It involves a famous son of our most rightward province, one Don Jamieson. Mr. Jamieson was a cabinet minister in the Trudeau government back in the 1960s and 1970s and as such was called upon from time to time to campaign through the Newfoundland outports. During one of those sorties he met a woman in her nineties who, his handlers informed Jamieson, had never been sick a day in her life.

"I find that remarkable, madame," said Jamieson. "Have you never been bedridden?"

The woman laughed merrily. "Oh, Lard, sir, yiss! T'ousands of times! And twice in a dory!"

Drop the H-Bomb

The human race has only one really effective weapon, and that is laughter.

—MARK TWAIN

Our increasingly Don Cherry-like federal government is in the process of laying out $9 billion for sixty-five fighter jets—that's $140 million per crate—for planes that critics claim are absurdly unsuited to Canada's needs.

But that's okay because Honest Sam, the fast-talking guy in the stovepipe hat who sold them to us, is throwing in a twenty-year service contract that will only cost us another $7 billion.

Sixteen billion dollars. I'm sure we could have hired Jon Stewart for way less than that.

Stewart is, of course, the host of the popular *Daily Show*, the TV news source for humour junkies who don't find *Fox News* sufficiently hilarious. *The Daily Show* skewers politicians, exposing them for the buffoons, poltroons and baboons that they so frequently are. Trouble is, the show's got so much American raw material from Washington, the Tea Party, Rick Perry, Michele Bachmann (and of course *Fox News*) it scarcely has time to train its crosshairs on its frostbitten neighbour to the north.

And that's a pity. Imagine what Stewart and his writers could do with walking punchlines like our pudgy pit bull Foreign Affairs Minister John Baird, the incoherent interim NDP leader Nycole Turmel and Defence Minister Peter "Just air-drop me at the lobster festival" MacKay. Not to mention Darth Harper.

Jon Stewart has only one arrow in his quiver—humour—but for the high and mighty, humour is the H-bomb, the ultimate weapon of mass distraction. Tyrants can weather insults, lies, treachery and chicanery but they cannot abide being laughed at.

And we don't laugh at them nearly often enough.

During the Second World War the most famous man on the planet was Adolf Hitler. The second most famous was an actor named Charlie Chaplin. Hitler loved Chaplin's films—until the actor made one called *The Great Dictator*, which lampooned Hitler. Hitler responded by putting Chaplin on his death list.

In 1989 when the Velvet Revolution swept through Czechoslovakia, peaceful protestors came up with the ultimate "up yours" to humiliate the occupying Soviet tyrants. Under cover of darkness they sneaked up to a massive public monument in a Czech square that featured a menacing Russian tank. They painted it fuchsia pink.

It is impossible to take a pink army tank seriously.

People are warming to this newfound weapon for the weaponless. In the decidedly undemocratic republic of Belarus, the head thug, Alexander Lukashenko, has recently outlawed applause.

That's because opponents of his regime have been holding "laugh-ins," wherein crowds of protestors mass in front of the presidential palace, break into huge grins and begin to applaud—apropos of nothing. Soon waves of laughter break out. It's irresistible. Eventually even the police join in.

Lukashenko goes bat shit crazy whenever this happens. His latest edict declares that anyone caught clapping on Belarus Independence Day will be arrested on the spot.

Can't help but smile, can you?

Canada has had its own political pricksters—Rick Mercer and Marg, Princess Warrior, have brought blushes to the well-upholstered cheeks of many an Ottawa trougher, but those platforms are getting creaky and showing their age. (Did you realize *This Hour Has 22 Minutes* is going on twenty years old?)

No, for real political humour with teeth you have to go to *The Daily Show* and its offshoot, *The Colbert Report*—even if the CanCon percentage is lamentably low.

Currently, Stephen Colbert is lampooning the stuffing out of the US campaign finance laws that Republican wheel-greasers and pork-barrellers have so thoroughly corrupted they've managed to get corporations declared "citizens." (Fred Exxon! C'mon over here and meet Bob Walmart!) That way there's no limit on how much said "citizens" can spend to elect their favourite candidate.

Stephen Colbert is steadfastly opposed to such skulduggery.

"I do not accept the status quo," Colbert fearlessly declares. Then adds: "I do accept Visa, MasterCard and American Express."

Castormania Forever

When someone writes about beavers, one assumes the person is a zoologist, works for a porn magazine, or is a Canadian.

—REINHOLD AMAN, US LINGUIST

I am a castormaniac. It's not my fault; it comes with the territory. I was born Canadian, I grew up Canadian, I live in Canada. Even more damning, I was weaned on a 1950s' TV sitcom called *Leave It to Beaver.* Ergo, my condition: castormania.

Castor refers, of course to *Castor canadensis*, aka the beaver. If you are Canadian you too are by definition stark staring beaver crazy.

Well, think about it. The beaver is our national animal. He was front and centre on our very first postage stamp, the Threepenny Beaver, issued in 1851. He is celebrated on the Hudson's Bay coat of arms, the crest of the Canadian Pacific Railway and the nickel in your pocket. Canada's first international press baron? Lord Beaverbrook. Our most famous aeronautical superstar? The de Havilland DHC-2 bush plane, better known as the Beaver. Where do Canucks buy the material to make a picnic table? Beaver Lumber. And what is a lad aged five to seven called in the Boy Scout movement? A Beaver. The chubby little rodent with the teeth like oversized Chiclets and the tail like a kitchen spatula permeates the very warp and woof of what it means to be Canadian.

And rightly so. If it weren't for the beaver, Canada wouldn't exist.

When early European explorers were drawn to the shores of Canada they came for the buckets of cod, the endless pods of whales offshore and the forests of arrow-straight pine and fir so perfect for shipbuilding. But they could access all that almost without leaving their ships. To get to the rich, thick beaver pelts so popular back in London and Paris they had to come inland and stay awhile. Come inland they did. Eventually those acquisitive trappers and traders paddled and trekked right across the country. Beaver fever made it all the way to the shores of the Pacific Ocean.

They nearly wiped out the beaver in the process but never mind. The critter is nothing if not fertile and beaver populations have rebounded nicely since European fops stopped wearing fur on their heads.

And we Canadians haven't forgotten our debt to the humble beaver. My, no. Why we even have a magazine dedicated to Canadian history— Mordecai Richler proclaimed it the best in the country—that bears the animal's name in the masthead. *The Beaver* has been proudly published out of Winnipeg for more than ninety years.

Oops, strike that. The editorial board recently announced that they are changing the title of the second-oldest magazine in the country from *The Beaver* to (yawn) *Canadian History Magazine.*

Why? You know why.

Because the name of Canada's most famous furry ambassador has been co-opted. Usurped. Stolen. Fact of the matter is, when you Google "beaver" on your laptop you don't get "historical publications"; you get . . . well, if you don't know, you really need to get out of the nunnery more often.

Canadian History Magazine—what a sad, grey, pusillanimous cop-out.

Fortunately, not all Canadian magazine people are so lacking in spunk. The folks in Vancouver who put out the literary magazine *Geist* announced that they were changing their name too—to *The Beaver.* Said editor-in-chief Stephen Osborne in a press release: "When we started *Geist*, we really wanted to name it after the wildlife that Canada is famous for but *The Beaver* was taken, Loon had gone to legal tender, Moosehead was all about beer and the Canada goose—well, that's just silly."

I was delighted that *Geist* was henceforth to be known as *The Beaver*—until I noticed the date on the press release: April 1.

Rats! (so to speak)—An April Fool's joke.

Back in the Middle Ages there was another magazine of sorts that was published from time to time. It was called a Bestiary—an encyclopedia of beasts, if you will. In it, medieval scholars wrote descriptions of virtually every animal that walked, flew over or slithered across the earth. The writers were not exactly slaves to truth and what they didn't know they didn't hesitate to make up. Of the beaver for instance, they wrote: "The beaver is hunted for its testicles, which are valued for making medicine. When the beaver sees that it cannot escape from the hunter, it bites off its testicles and throws them to the hunter, who then stops pursuing the beaver. If another hunter chases the beaver, it shows the hunter that it has already lost its testicles and so is spared."

Doesn't sound like any beaver I know.

Sounds more like a description of the editors of *Canadian History Magazine*.

Of All the Luck

A h, yes. Good old, bad old, Dirty Harry, squinting down the barrel of his handgun cannon and giving the killer/kidnapper/psycho one last shot at macho redemption. Is Harry's gun empty? Maybe, maybe not. If it is, his opponent only has to pick up his piece and blow Harry away. Killer/kidnapper/psycho decides that he does, in fact, feel lucky; he goes for his gun.

It doesn't work out for him.

Well, luck's a funny thing. Sometimes you're the windshield, as my pappy used to say, and sometimes you're the bug.

Except when you're all windshield, like Joan Ginther of Bishop, Texas. Last spring she won $10 million with a scratch-off ticket in a Texas lottery. "Oh, goody," thought Ms. Ginther. "I can put that with the $3 million I won in the 2008 lottery. And the $2 million I won in 2006. Not to mention the $5.4 million I won in 1993."

True story. Experts say you've got a better shot at being fricasseed by a lightning bolt than you have of winning a lottery. Joan Ginther's been struck by Fate's Golden Forefinger four times in the past two decades.

Unlike Chris Tarttelin. He's a thirty-seven-year-old Brit trying to become a Canadian. He figured he'd won the Life Lottery when he moved to Saskatoon with his wife and two kids two years ago. He's a computer software developer and he'd already lined up a good job—just the kind of new blood you'd think we'd bend over backwards to attract. All he had to do was pass a routine medical exam and he was in.

Oops.

Turns out Mr. Tarttelin couldn't pass the medical exam. He suffers from one grievous personal handicap that renders him unfit for Canadian citizenship.

He's too honest.

When asked if he'd ever taken drugs, Tarttelin replied, "I tried pot as a teenager but I didn't really take to it. I tried it a couple of times and that was about it."

Wrong answer. Tarttelin was told he would have to have a psychiatric assessment. What's more he'd have to have the assessment done and a report from the psychiatrist within sixty days. "You can't see a psychiatrist in Saskatoon in that time frame," says Tarttelin. He's moving back to Britain with his family.

The level of hypocrisy here is truly mind-boggling. A psychiatric assessment for a couple of joints smoked nineteen years ago? If that's valid 98 percent of Canadians should be on the couch or living at the funny farm. Barack Obama tried pot. So did Arnold Schwarzenegger, Ted Turner, Stephen King and Sir Richard Branson. Pierre Berton went on Rick Mercer's TV show and delivered a joint-rolling tutorial. He was in his eighties!

And those are just the famous folks who manned up and owned it. (Still not inhaling, Bill Clinton?) I venture to guess that the Citizenship and Immigration buzzards who vetoed Tarttelin's bid for Canadian citizenship themselves toked up a time or two in their lives.

Lesson for all prospective Canadian immigrants: if you admit to so much as sniffing a cannabis leaf you're history.

Liars and cheaters, however, are welcome.

It all comes down to luck in the end, and its Chris Tarttelin's bad luck to be unusually honest. "I'm a painfully honest person. It doesn't occur to me to answer questions any other way."

Loser. We don't need your kind in Canada. Why don't you try Germany? They're more tolerant of over-indulgers there. As evidenced by the thirty-five-year-old Polish immigrant who moved to Bochum, Germany, five years ago. Recently he went to the doctor to have a cyst removed from the back of his head.

The doctor removed a bullet instead.

Confronted with the lead nugget the guy dimly recalled receiving a blow to the head at a New Year's party "in 2004 or 2005."

He told the doctor he didn't remember it all that clearly because he had been "very stoned."

Talk about dumb luck.

Happy Haiti? Hopefully

Consider the letter "H."

Such a sturdy little one-rung ladder of a letter. A harbinger, too, of hardy, healthful words beginning with H. Ten-dollar words like harmony, hospitality and heartfelt. Simple words like haven, home and hearth.

And of course, happy.

But then there's Haiti.

Also an "H" word but hardly a happy one. Not long ago a devastating earthquake reduced what was already a basket case of a country to something beyond and beneath horrible.

Sounds blasphemous, but there's an upside to what happened in Haiti. It moved us. Hard on the heels of the terrible news came a massive, spontaneous outpouring, a global unvoiced chorus of "What can we do?" And nowhere deeper or stronger than from Canada. Even Bill Clinton was flabbergasted. "It has been unbelievable," said the ex-US president. "The Canadian people are so generous. I'll bet you on a per-capita basis they're number one in the world helping Haiti."

That was the amazing part—the "per capita." The millions that flowed from the coffers of Ottawa could be taken for granted—that's just how Canada behaves on the world stage. What was not foreseen was the response from ordinary Canucks. Tins and jars appeared on office desks and by cash registers, all marked "For Haiti." Anonymous citizens emptied their purses, tossed in crumpled fivers and ten-spots or scribbled hefty cheques. Kids in classrooms across the land chipped in their loonies and toonies.

A lady I barely know emailed me a shaky, raw video that a boyfriend of her niece had put together. The video, of Port au Prince before and after, was amateurish, slapdash and utterly heartbreaking. It told you where to send money and we did. We had to.

The firefighters at our local fire hall put out an empty fireman's helmet on the fender of the town fire truck. They collected $6,000 the first weekend.

We could even text financial aid to Haiti on our cellphones. Tens of thousands of Canadians thumbed it in. For those of us less technically dextrous, Google works. Typing "Haiti Relief" into the search box gets you more than forty million hits. We'll never know the real total, but ordinary Canadians have ponied up at least $220 million for Haiti. That's not counting the food, the clothing, the medicine or the soldiers and civilians who gave their expertise and sweat equity on the ground.

Haiti remains devastated, but after decades—centuries, really—of paralysis, it's stirring. For the first time in memory, Haitians can dare to—another "H" word—hope.

The Haitian disaster may even make the world a happier place. A recent University of Virginia study asked the question: What makes us happy? It discovered, for starters, a lot of things that don't.

It doesn't help to be filthy rich. It makes no difference if you're brilliant. A retiree in Victoria is no happier than a plumber in Iqaluit. It doesn't really matter if you look like Johnny Depp or Quasimodo, Jennifer Lopez or Susan Boyle. It's immaterial if you're younger than springtime or older than dirt.

What matters, happiness-wise, is that you give.

A pint of blood or a spare kidney, a benefit concert at Massey Hall or an afternoon each week sorting clothes at the Sally Ann thrift shop. A loonie in a wino's ball cap or a million-dollar endowment to your alma mater.

Or help for Haiti.

It's our choice. We can spend our spare cash on boob lifts, Cartier watches, golf club memberships or back-to-back round the world cruises, but we all know in our ("H" word alert) heart of hearts it won't work.

Giving works. It makes you . . . happy.

Speaking of "H" words: That study I mentioned is entitled *The Happiness Hypothesis*. Name of the author?

Haidt. Jonathan Haidt.

Holy Hannah. Or, if you prefer: Hallelujah.

Java Jive

They drink an awful lot of coffee in Brazil.

—Venerable song lyric

No doubt—but they also drink an awful lot of coffee in Brampton, Brandon, Brockville and Berthierville, QC. We Canucks like our coffee. In my hometown, which is a small one, I can count four coffee houses within a sugar cube's toss of one another, not one of them a franchise. I bet it's the same story where you live. When it comes to enthusiasm for downing mugs of java, Canucks are dedicated slurpers, eight out of ten of us drinking the beverage at least occasionally. On a daily basis more Canadians (63 percent) indulge than Americans (49 percent). We may not be as wired as Finlanders who manage to process twelve kilos of the stuff per capita per annum, but we're way ahead of dainty dabblers in the UK, Australia, France and Germany.

And Canada has made a seminal contribution to worldwide coffee culture. We gave the world Tim Hortons.

Man, I'm so old I can remember when Tim Horton was a Maple Leaf defenceman. (Hell, I'm so old I can remember when Toronto had a hockey team—but I digress.)

What started as a dinky donut shop in Hamilton nearly half a century ago has blossomed into an international powerhouse with outlets in virtually every town and city in the country, plus twelve US states. You can find a Tim Hortons in places as various as Michigan and Kentucky, Rhode Island and West Virginia. There's even one in Kandahar.

Needless to say, not everyone—even in Canada—is a fan of Tim Hortons coffee. Indeed, caffeine freaks tend to split into one of two camps: the Tim Hortons crowd or the Starbucks fraternity. Broadly speaking, Tim's is blue collar while Starbucks is uptown. Tim's is fluorescent lighting and plastic tables; Starbucks is overstuffed sofas, MoMA wall posters and Norah Young soundtracks. At Tim's you see plenty of customers with trucker's wallets sticking out of their back pocket; Starbucks customers tend more toward laptops and newspapers folded to the *New York Times* crossword.

Oh yeah, and one more thing: Tim's is cheap; Starbucks, not so much.

I'm a touch schizophrenic when it comes to coffee loyalty. I'm more likely to pop into a Tim Hortons than a Starbucks. It's not the clangy, high school cafeteria ambiance that attracts me. It's knowing I can get what I want without a lot of screwing around.

I don't want a six-dollar vanilla crème doppio half-caff foamless soy latte Frappuccino, and it'll be a frosty Friday in downtown Hades before I order a venti anything. I just want a cup of frickin' coffee.

A cynic might say that I'm missing the point—that Starbucks is not about selling coffee, it's about selling a lifestyle. They might argue that what Starbucks is offering is a non-hostile, predictable, ever-so-slightly snobby haven for the upwardly mobile to hide in.

How else can you charge six bucks for a mystery beverage that's mostly hot water? Perhaps customers are catching on. Starbucks closed nearly 700 outlets in 2008. Last year they closed another 300 and laid off 6,700 workers. The company's latest attempt to stay relevant saw the opening of a Starbucks café that doesn't call itself Starbucks. It calls itself—for reasons best known to company marketing geniuses—"15th Avenue and Tea." And yes, it features an in-house "Tea Master" available for solemn consultations.

One other sign of apparent desperation in the Starbucks family: the decision to allow customers to carry firearms openly (in the twenty-nine states where it's legal to do so) into their local Starbucks.

Now there's an attractive consumer option: sipping coffee next to an America Firster jacked up on a double espresso and wearing a Glock Nine on his hip.

Sounds to me like a corporation that's circling the drain—unlike Tim Hortons, which just keeps getting bigger. The Canadian company has announced plans to open 900 new US outlets in the next three years (they've already got over 3,000 across Canada and they hope to add 1,000 more).

Imagine. Of all the percolated coffee served in Canada 77 percent comes out of a Tim Hortons coffee pot. They serve 1.5 billion customers every year.

Not bad, for a business scheme brewed up in the head of a hockey player who patrolled the blue line nearly fifty years ago.

The Unsinkable Tubby Black

This column is about Conrad Moffat Black, OK, KCSG, PC, aka Lord Black of Crossharbour, not to mention Mogul, Tycoon, Poobah, Master of the Universe and Convicted Felon. This man is no relation to A. Black, Esq. The scribbler of this column is perfectly okay with that.

I do not care for Conrad Black for a multitude of reasons but chief among them stems from a conversation I had years ago with a Quebec journalist. At the time Conrad was acquiring small Canadian dailies and weeklies like a Monopoly player on crack. My friend was a columnist and a veteran of two Conradian takeovers. He told me the phrase Conrad Black used to describe the inevitable flurry of firings and dismissals that occurred whenever Conrad assumed control of a newspaper. Black, smiling, called the procedure "drowning the puppies." As a newspaper lover and a dog fancier, that humour was just a little too Black, even for me.

Conrad Black is easy to dislike. He is arrogant, boastful, pompous and utterly contemptuous of all lesser beings, which is pretty well everyone this side of the Pope. As a newspaper proprietor he even sneered at newspaper people. In a submission to a Canadian Senate committee, Black, characteristically employing the royal "we," sniffed:

"We must express the view, based on our empirical observations, that a substantial number of journalists are ignorant, lazy, opinionated, and intellectually dishonest. The profession is heavily cluttered with aged hacks toiling through a miasma of mounting decrepitude and often alcoholism, and even more so with arrogant and abrasive youngsters who substitute 'commitment' for insight." So much for his colleagues. His enemies fared worse. He called the Bishop of Calgary "a jumped up twerp" and his business partner David Ratner "the rat." He dismissed the US vice-president as a "mendacious hypocrite." He belittled his own investors as "a bunch of self-righteous hypocrites and ingrates."

Mr. Black is fond of calling people hypocrites. Interesting, coming from a man who tossed off his Canadian citizenship like a used Kleenex when a British knighthood winked in his direction.

Not surprisingly, Conrad Black became a giant neocon piñata for legions of journalists who didn't have to work for him—and for many who did. The now-defunct Canadian satirical magazine *Frank* dubbed him "Tubby" after Tubby Tompkins, a character in the *Little Lulu* comic strip. Tubby Tompkins was a rotund, nasty and scheming child of privilege who often became a victim of his own shortcomings. The analogy stuck.

Not that Conrad ever gave a rap. He was mega-bright, he was filthy rich and he was utterly impervious to the potshots and put-downs that percolated up from the little people. He had money, fame and fortune.

And then the roof fell in.

Lord Black of Crossharbour ended up swatting mosquitoes in a cell in a Florida jail. Never in my lifetime has any mortal fallen so far and so utterly.

But here's the thing.

Conrad Black was not beaten. He served his time like a pro. He never cried the blues or begged for mercy or murmured contrition. He spent $100 million on his defence; still faces over $1 billion in civil suits—and yet the man is unbowed.

Is he magnificent—or deluded?

Maybe he just has *sisu* in spades. *Sisu* is a Finnish word that means, roughly, extraordinary bravery and tenacity. The Finns showed *sisu* when they fought the militarily superior Russians to a standstill in the Second World War. I once asked a Finlander to explain *sisu* to me. "It means having the hide of a rhinoceros," he told me. Then, after a pause he added:

"And perhaps the brain of one too."

What's in a Name?

*It is important for us, my brothers, that we exterminate
from our lands this nation which seeks only to destroy
us. You see as well as I that we can no longer supply our
needs . . . Therefore, my brothers, we must all swear their
destruction and wait no longer. Nothing prevents us; they
are few in numbers, and we can accomplish it.*

Obwandiyag, chief of the Ottawas, was no friend of the British—
that was the nation that he was advocating for extermination. He
did his best to make it happen too. Obwandiyag and his warriors laid
siege to the British fort at Detroit and massacred a British detachment
at the Battle of Bloody Run nearby.

Was Obwandiyag American or Canadian? Older than both. He
lived and fought back in the mid-1700s along what would one day
become the Ontario–Michigan border. He was decades in advance of
the American Declaration of Independence and a century before the
notion of a nation called Canada began to float about.

Oh, and one other thing: Obwandiyag had another name. Pontiac.

I didn't learn any of the above in class. In my school years teachers
of Canadian history treated the entire aboriginal presence as colourful
but slightly inconvenient background to the story of the founding of
Canada. We learned little of Native customs, traditions and way of life,
nor of the fact that when we whiteys arrived they'd already lived on this
continent for milliennia.

For me as a kid Pontiac wasn't a fierce warrior. It was a blue and
black 1952 two-door sedan.

It was my dad's first car and I learned to drive in it. There was a headlight dimmer switch on the floor beside the clutch (look it up, youngsters), a stick shift on the steering column and no power anything, although it did have air conditioning—provided you cranked the windows down.

It was a boringly conventional, resolutely bourgeois buggy. The only hint of the aboriginal origin of its name was the hood ornament—a stylized, Art Deco-style Indian head that may or may not have looked like Pontiac the man—no authenticated drawings or paintings of him survive.

Even the Indian-head icon would disappear as Pontiacs underwent a radical transformation in the 1960s and 1970s. It stopped being the Car Your Father Drove and mutated into a roaring, low-slung, over-powered "muscle car" favoured by high-testosterone, low-browed young males. Guys with mullets and vocabularies that peaked at around twenty words, most of them blue. Guys who thought gold chains, Fu Manchu moustaches and tattooed knuckles were killer fashion statements.

Pontiac was the brand that invented the muscle car and nobody made them louder, faster or more in-your-face down and dirty.

And they sold like cold beer in a heat wave.

"Sportier than a Chevrolet but less uppity than an Oldsmobile or Buick," is what the Pontiac car ads promised and for years the company surfed a rich wave of customer loyalty.

But car manufacturers are born tinkerers. They love to fix things even if they aren't broken (remember Edsel?). Somewhere in the mid-1980s the big thinkers who gave the world GTOs, Firebirds and Trans Ams got restless and decided it was time for Pontiac to undergo a "brand re-think." They summoned their designers and engineers and instructed them to come up with the Next Big Thing.

They came up with a lot of things, among them a minivan called the Montana that looked like a bread truck, and later a "cross-over" compact called the Aztek. Do you remember the Aztek? Probably not. It was around just long enough to win the coveted *Daily Telegraph* title of Ugliest Car of All Time.

Perhaps the car was doomed from the start—its creators couldn't even spell "Aztec" correctly.

The Aztek was the beginning of a death spiral for Pontiac. That spiral ended in a flush October 2010 when General Motors announced that after eighty-four years and forty million cars the brand was officially dead. The world would see no more automobiles with the word Pontiac on the grille.

Chief Obwandiyag can finally have his other name back.

Calling a Spade a Shovel

Euphemism: the substitution of an agreeable or inoffensive expression for one that may offend or suggest something unpleasant.

—MERRIAM-WEBSTER DICTIONARY

Euphemism is a euphemism for lying.

—BOBBIE GENTRY

I have to go along with Ms. Gentry on this one. There is something inherently weasel-ish and underhanded about the average euphemism. It's a masquerading device designed to cushion the sting and befog the truth. Hence, people don't "die"; they "pass over," "buy the farm," "cash in their chips" or "go to their reward." Even Mafiosi get mealy-mouthed when it comes to talking about death. When mobsters whack a stoolie and dump his body in the river, he isn't dead, he's "sleeping with the fishes."

Used to be if a junkie got caught with your television set under his arm he'd be arrested and thrown in jail. But we don't have junkies anymore, we have "substance abusers." We also don't have jails; they've been replaced by "correctional facilities."

We don't even have television sets anymore. Now they're "home entertainment suites."

Old folks, coots and codgers? Sorry, they're now "senior citizens" or, more excruciatingly, "golden agers." Pornography? That's been upgraded to "adult entertainment."

Please. Glen Gould, Margaret Atwood, the Group of Seven—that's adult entertainment. A skin flick is just a skin flick.

As for baseball, you don't have to be way out in left field to recognize the game as a gold mine for euphemisms—especially euphemisms of the sexual persuasion. If you "hit it off" with that cute stranger down the bar with the right "pitch," chances are you'll "hit a homer" before the night is done. On the other hand, if you don't keep your eye on the ball or you get your signals crossed you could strike out without even getting to first base. Oh well. You can always console yourself with the notion that the object of your affection was probably a switch hitter, perhaps even playing for the other team.

Politicians would probably wither up and die of asphyxiation without euphemisms. These people don't spend taxpayers' money, they "invest in Canada's future." They don't drill for oil, they "explore for energy sources." George W. Bush, an otherwise dim and spectacularly unqualified president, was positively poetic when it came to spinning euphemisms. The Bushies gave America the Clean Air Initiative—which permitted power plants to release more air pollution. They also created the Healthy Forest Initiative—which sanctioned increased cutting of trees.

Actually, I malign the man. George Bush didn't create those euphemisms, a staff flunky did. George was busy cutting brush at the time.

But Bush wasn't in the same league as that master of flannelmouthing, Richard M. Nixon. When a reporter caught Nixon in a flat-out lie, Nixon furrowed his brow, waved an admonitory forefinger and intoned, "That explanation is currently inoperative."

Ah, but no agency taps the BS potential of the euphemism as thoroughly and exhaustively as the military. They're the folks who turned invasions into "police actions," civilian butchery into "collateral damage," assassination into "termination with extreme prejudice." And look at the linguistic sleight of hand they've done when it comes to describing what the horrors of war can do to the mind of a soldier.

In the First World War it was called "shell shock"—but that was a little too, well . . . real. By the Second World War the approved term was "battle fatigue."

Still a little too close to the bone. During the Korean War the term for the condition was massaged down to "operational exhaustion."

Still a little raw. Today the label for those wretched grunts who return from war with hollow eyes, nightmare memories and permanently jangled nervous systems? Oh, they're just down with a touch of "post-traumatic stress disorder."

Euphemisms can be used to hide a lot of ugly truths—and that's not always a bad thing. There was that case of the nineteenth-century ne'er-do-well son of a rich London family who was banished to Canada with a small allowance in the hope that he would get his act together. Unfortunately, Canada didn't change him. He was a drunk and a thief and he ended his days at the end of a rope in Alberta. The judge who presided at his hanging felt no need to bring more shame on the man's family but it was his duty to inform them of his demise. His letter to the family included this explanation: "We regret to inform you of the passing of your son. He was participating in a public ceremony when the platform on which he was standing suddenly gave way."

Getting Rich—An Optical Illusion

The word of the day is "optics." My dictionary defines it as the branch of physics that studies the properties of light, but there's a trippier definition currently in circulation. "Optics" can stand for "public image." Rick Hansen: good optics. Tiger Woods: not so good optics.

Then there's the Royal Bank of Canada. RBC spent a fortune during the 2010 Winter Olympics on ads showing what a caring, sharing and fiscally prudent company they are. Just the people you'd want to shepherd your hard-earned nickels and toonies wisely. Good optics.

Unlike the story that appeared in the *Globe and Mail*—the one telling how Gord Nixon, chief executive of the Royal Bank of Canada, got a paycheque for $10.4 million in 2009.

Mr. Nixon must be getting better at his job. He only managed to pull down $8.8 million the year before. Call me Chicken Little, but when I see the head teller of my bank raking in an annual salary worthy of a Saudi oil bandit I check to see if my wallet's still in my pocket.

Thing is, Mr. Nixon wasn't even RBC's biggest financial make-out meister. Mark Standish, who runs RBC Capital Markets, pocketed $14 million for 2009. Doug McGregor his co-pilot had to make do with $13 million.

So RBC's top three guys saw fit to steam shovel nearly $38 million into their own pockets for a year's work—and they think I should invest my money with them????

Sorry, boys—bad optics.

And lest you think this is the beginning of a Big Bad Banks rant, let me hasten to point out that not all Canadian banks are equal. Why, over at the Canadian Imperial Bank of Commerce the head honcho actually made $2 million *less* than he did a year previous. That's right—Gerry McCaughey, CIBC's chief executive, was forced to stumble through the year under a 25 percent pay cut.

Don't send Mr. McCaughey a care package just yet. The CIBC treasury still managed to scrape up an annual stipend of $6.24 million to keep the wolf from the boss's door.

Enron, Goldman Sachs, Bernie Madoff, Canada's own Earl Jones . . . the parade of corporate greedheads marches on, dragging their loot bags behind them. There was a time when such sackers and pillagers would have had the decency to at least wear an eye patch and a peg leg, but today they come at us in pinstripes and BMWs. Did you know by twelve noon of January 3 Canada's top one hundred CEOs had each earned the equivalent of an average Canadian's annual wage? That's right; by lunch time January 3 (Canada's first working day) our highest paid bosses had already pocketed $42,305 apiece—174 times more than the average Canadian working stiff.

Money means different things to different people. H.L. Hunt opined that it really wasn't all that important. "Money's just a way of keeping score," Hunt said. You can say things like that when, like Hunt, you've got $800 million or so in the bank. He might be right though, because there has to be a limit to the toys and diversions a mortal can actually use. How do you justify a multi-million dollar salary when you see Haitian kids with flies in their eyes?

And then there's Joshua Silver. He's no corporate wheeler-dealer, just a professor of physics at Oxford University. Still, he's arrived. He could spend the rest of his career turning out incomprehensible papers and sipping sherry with the dons.

Instead he's working on refining his invention—Adspecs. They're eyeglasses—eyeglasses that will change the world we live in. Look around at all the people with specs on. Now imagine living in a land where all those folks are barefaced. They'd still need the glasses, you understand—they just couldn't afford to buy them. Experts reckon there are a billion people out there who are too poor to afford the corrective eyewear they need.

That's where Joshua Silver's Adspecs come in. The eyeglasses he invented feature lenses filled with silicone that can be adjusted by syringes attached to the frames. Long story short, people who wear

Adspecs can dial their own eye prescriptions to suit themselves, no optometrist, ophthalmologist or optician necessary.

Dr. Silver could make himself a mega millionaire by charging top dollar for eyeglasses like that. Instead he's figuring out ways to make them cheaper. He's got the price down to $20 a pair but he wants to get it down to just a dollar—and then he hopes to donate boxcar loads of them to aid organizations around the world. He's already sent off more than 30,000 pairs to Africa.

That's good optics. Royal Bank of Canada, please copy.

PART FIVE

Who's in Charge Here?

Legalize Pot? Weed Be Better Off

I love the concept of the tipping point—the idea that there can be a single moment in time when one last critical molecule of resistance crumbles and the whole damn mountainside comes down. Egypt recently found its political tipping point. Rosa Parks was a tipping point for racial discrimination in America. That Tunisian fruit seller who set fire to himself and ignited the Arab Spring was a political tipping point.

I believe another tipping point was reached recently in Missoula County, Montana.

A kid by the name of Touray Cornell faced a felony charge: possession of an illegal substance punishable by serious prison time. The substance: marijuana, found by a police raid on his home. The amount: one-sixteenth of an ounce.

One-sixteenth of an ounce equals less than two grams. Too little to roll in a cigarette paper. You could be carrying one-sixteenth of an ounce of pot around in your pant cuff right now and not even know it. But Touray Cornell was charged and he was going down, just as soon as Dusty Deschamps, district judge for Missoula County, could select a jury.

Er . . . small problem. When each prospective juror learned what the case was about and how much "drug" was involved they refused to serve. Juror after juror told the judge they would refuse to convict anyone over such a miniscule amount of pot. Twenty-seven prospective jurors were polled; twenty-two of them said that not only would they not convict but that the whole farce was "a waste of taxpayer money." "It's a mutiny," wailed the district attorney.

High time, too. The war on marijuana has been going on for a hundred years, give or take. It is impossible to calculate the Himalayas of money, man hours and human grief it's cost, but the price tag is surely in the hundreds of billions of dollars, the lives blighted too numerous to comprehend.

And the result? When I was a youth you pretty much had to be on a first-name basis with a jazz musician if you wanted to score some pot. Nowadays? Just hang out around any schoolyard or shopping mall and look interested. The grade eight connection will find you.

Historians in the future will shake their heads to learn there was a time when people could spend years behind bars for possession of a barnyard weed. Get caught with a baggie in your backpack in jurisdictions like Texas and life as you know it is over, but even in BC-Bud-happy Canada you pay a heavy price. There are three people in my life who have criminal records and hence cannot cross the US–Canada border. Ever. Their offence? They were caught—three or four decades ago—with a joint in their pocket or a couple of roaches in the car ashtray.

Well, they could get across if they were willing to pay a $5,000 bribe to the US government to look the other way, but that's another shakedown story.

Most of the blame for Canadian hysteria over marijuana can be laid at the feet of a single Albertan, Ms. Emily F. Murphy of Edmonton. Ms. Murphy, a juvenile court judge back in the 1920s, wrote under the pen name "Janey Canuck" for *Maclean's* magazine.

And she spewed some truly astounding crap. She wrote—and *Maclean's* published—that all marijuana users were "non-white and non-Christian, wanting only to seduce white women."

"Behind these dregs of humanity," she wrote, "is an international conspiracy of yellow and black drug pushers whose ultimate goal is the domination of the bright-browed races of the world."

One "fix" of the demon weed, Ms. Murphy assured her readers, "has the effect of driving (smokers) completely insane. The addicts lose all sense of moral responsibility and are immune to pain . . . become raving maniacs, liable to kill or indulge in any form of violence using the most savage cruelty."

Murphy's Palinesque ravings turned into a best-selling book and—incredibly—influenced Canadian law. Marijuana was declared illegal, its possession punishable by jail time. "A decision was made without any scientific basis, nor even any real sense of urgency, placing cannabis on the same basis as the opiate narcotics, and it has remained so to this day." So said Justice Gerald LeDain in his Royal Commission of 1972.

That's nearly forty years ago. Canadians can still get a record for pot possession.

I wonder if we'll ever become as brave as those jurors in Missoula County.

Common Sense: Lost in the Sun

Ah, the sacred rites of spring! A balmy late afternoon on a baseball diamond in a leafy downtown park in Hamilton, Ontario; to the west, the sun slowly sinking like a syrupy golden ball. A bunch of the lads, middle-aged amateurs all, playing through the bottom of the eighth. Look! There's George Black on the infield. A burly, bushy-bearded guy who runs his own trucking business is George, but tonight he's patrolling the third-base bag, as he has in this league for years.

No World Series heebie-jeebies here. No textbook double plays or ninety-mile-an-hour split-fingered fastballs. The game is slo-pitch, so the guy on the mound doesn't so much hurl the ball as lob it loopily toward home plate. The batter tenses, swings and . . . lines the ball straight at George, playing third.

George doesn't catch it. He "loses it in the sun," as the old sportscaster's cliché goes, for indeed the sun is setting behind the backstop. Astronomically speaking, the batter represents old Sol, George is the Earth and the ball is the moon between the two, invisible in a miniature solar eclipse.

Planet Earth (which is to say George) throws up his glove hand, but too late. The screaming line drive slams into his hand fracturing two fingers then deflecting into George's sunglasses, shattering them and cutting George for twenty stitches around the eyes.

George Black may not be a professional ballplayer but he is an alert and canny citizen of our times. He reads the situation and reacts just like a pro. He knows instinctively what to do.

He sues.

Not the batter. Not the pitcher. Not the amateur league he plays in. George sues . . . Dofasco, the company that paid for and erected the baseball facilities on which George got injured. His reasoning? Impeccable. Dofasco should have had the foresight to erect a screen protecting players from the setting sun.

In the lawsuit Dofasco is charged with "failing to warn (Mr. Black) of the dangers of the sun at the particular time of day." George himself puts it more succinctly: "There have been no instructions (from Dofasco) in avoiding the sun."

George reckons $1.5 million would assuage his grief and suffering.

Good point. I know when I got that bad sunburn at Tofino last year I didn't get so much as a sympathy card from the BC government much less a cash settlement.

And remember that woman who successfully sued McDonald's a few years back for her burned crotch? She'd purchased a coffee in the McDonald's drive-thru, placed it between her thighs while she drove away and the coffee slopped over and burned her. Burned her! Obviously it was the restaurant's fault for serving superheated coffee. Heartless bastards.

There is some precedent for George's baseball-oriented lawsuit. In 1985 an aggrieved mother sued Exhibition Place in Toronto after her ten-year-old son was hit by a foul ball during a Blue Jays game.

She lost. Back then, judges—even some citizens—subscribed to the theory that Stuff Happens and that occasionally it was the citizen's responsibility to Get Over It.

Today, George's lawsuit proceeds apace through the Canadian legal system. Dofasco has been compelled to hire Paul Jorgenson, an American architect who has designed several ball fields across North America. Mr. Jorgenson pointed out that most ball fields, like the one George Black was injured on, are designed so that the setting sun shines away from the batter's eyes, which means that once in a while it's going to shine into the eyes of at least some of the opposing players on the field. He also pointed out that it would be impractical, if not impossible, to shield the eyes of all infield players at all times. He did not add that ballplayers have been performing under these onerous conditions pretty much without complaint for the past century and a half or so.

The judge's response? He sided with . . . George. Dofasco's motion to dismiss was tossed and the case could now go to court. My guess is

Dofasco will sigh and settle out of court for some lesser amount. George Black will take home a bundle and the city of Hamilton will never see another Dofasco dime for recreational facilities in the city.

We all live and learn. And George, if you're reading this, here's something you might learn. You know how Dofasco failed to warn you "of the dangers of the sun at the particular time of day"? Here's a tip: This evening, sometime after supper and before it gets really dark . . . the sun will probably do it again.

Not for certain, but that's been the pattern every day for the past 4.5 billion years.

You might want to make a note of that and Scotch tape it to your baseball glove.

Hazards of the Workplace

Somewhere in the ocean of radio waves that bathe our planet there is an inspired and iconic bit of music hall nonsense called "The Bricklayer's Report." It is a humorous monologue first voiced by a British entertainer named Gerald Hoffnung back in 1958. It's been floating in the ether and delighting English-speakers ever since.

The piece purports to be a verbatim request for workman's compensation from a British bricklayer injured on the job. His feckless account of attempting to lower a barrel of bricks from the roof of a six-storey building, being yanked skyward by the too-heavy barrel, then plunged earthwards by the suddenly lighter barrel, then smashed senseless by the descending . . . oh, it's no use. My words can't do it justice. Google Gerald Hoffnung and listen to the irresistible original.

The Brits are awfully good at depicting hapless citizens grimly clinging to those last tattered shreds of dignity. Think of Peter Sellers' Inspector Clouseau. Think of the Monty Python gang. Think of clueless but ever-stiff-upper-lipped Basil, proprietor of Fawlty Towers.

Turns out that British thespians don't have to go all that far to find raw material for such depictions. Consider the on-the-job adventures of Peter Aspinall, a handyman who lives in Bolton, England, and works— or used to work—for a luxury hotel called Egerton House. Mr. Aspinall was asked to remove a large branch from a tree on the hotel grounds. Enthusiastically, he propped his ladder up against the branch, scampered up the rungs and commenced to saw.

Mr. Aspinall's mastery of arboreal modification was less than perfect. His understanding of the law of gravity was no hell either. Mr. Aspinall chose to make his cut between the ladder and the tree proper. Mr. Aspinall and the severed branch hit the ground approximately simultaneously.

Our not-so-handy handyman salvaged no comedic monologue from his mishap. Instead he limped off to a solicitor who obligingly filed a suit on his behalf against Egerton House. There's no word yet on the outcome of Aspinall's suit, but it doesn't look good for the hotel. The establishment has already been fined more than $3,000 after government health and safety inspectors pronounced it guilty of not carrying out a risk assessment on the limb-cutting assignment before turning Aspinall and his saw loose on the tree. Hotel management, said the investigators, should have informed Aspinall that it could be potentially dangerous to set one's ladder against a branch one proposes to cut down. The hotel also, opined the investigators, ought to have counselled their employee to engage and train an apprentice to hold and properly place the ladder.

The British minions of justice may provide a safe haven for the thick of head and the un-fleet of foot but they are no friends to fiendish criminals. Rodney Knowles learned that the hard way. There he was, driving home from a pub in Devon, England, when the flashing blue lights of a police cruiser suddenly bloomed in his rear-view mirror. The officers accused him of drunk driving but a roadside Breathalyzer showed he was sober. Still, the police sensed something . . . sinister. On a hunch, they opened the car's glove compartment and—AHA! There it was, nestled in a leather pouch, ready to wreak mayhem and horror on an unsuspecting populace. Mr. Knowles was arrested and charged with possession of an offensive weapon.

To wit: one Swiss Army knife.

A Swiss Army knife—the nerdiest of personal lifestyle accessories this side of a vinyl pocket protector. Millions of Swiss Army knives are sold annually in countries around the world. They are purchased by campers, hikers, Cub scouts, do-it-yourselfers and assorted gizmo and gadget freaks. I know this. I carry one myself. I also know that no airplane has ever been hijacked, no bank has ever been robbed, no hostage standoffs have ever been instigated or civilian massacres perpetrated by desperadoes wielding Swiss Army knives.

In any case, Mr. Knowles hardly fits the standard desperado profile. The man has never been in trouble with the law in his life; he's sixty-one years old and walks with the aid of a cane. He explained in court that his primary use for his Swiss Army knife was slicing apples on picnics. That defence cut no ice with the magistrates who found him guilty, fined him the equivalent of $100, gave him a "conditional discharge" and confiscated the "weapon" (which can be purchased at virtually any hardware or outfitter's store by any customer regardless of age or gender).

"It's a stupid law," said Mr. Knowles. "Now I have a criminal record."

Indeed it is, Mr. Knowles. Have you thought of contacting Gerald Hoffnung? Perhaps he could work it up into a comic monologue.

Manners Maketh (Wo)man

The age of chivalry is gone. That of the sophisters,
economists and calculators, has succeeded; and the glory of
Europe is extinguished forever.

Edmund Burke wrote those words back in 1790 and the chivalry he mourned was one we wouldn't recognize today. He was referring to the qualities expected of an ideal knight: exceptional courage, dedication to honour and justice, a readiness to always help the weak and disadvantaged.

Over the next couple of centuries the concept of chivalry devolved to become a loose code of manners for the boys—gentlemanliness, if you will—and most particularly, courteous behaviour toward women.

I'm not as old as Edmund Burke but close enough—and that's the way I was raised. I was taught to treat the cloven members of the human race with more deference than the crested ones. I learned early on that it was okay to roughhouse with Pat and Mike but not with Patricia and Michelle. I could swap dirty jokes with the guys but not the girls. It became second nature to hold open doors, surrender my seat on the bus or subway and to offer to carry the parcels of anyone who looked like they could use a hand.

Sounds quaintly innocent now. Back in the newly liberated 1970s such behaviour almost got me lynched.

I remember my first re-education lesson. It was circa 1973, I was approaching the front door of the CBC studios in Thunder Bay and a woman I knew slightly was coming behind me. Instinctively (suavely, I thought) I grasped the door handle, stepped back out of the way and gestured for the woman to enter.

She unloaded a tirade on my head that could have blistered paint.

I don't recall all the words she said. "Condescending" was in there for sure, and I think I heard something about "paternalistic superiority" and "centuries of male oppression."

The gist of her sermon was: I can open my own damned doors, thank you very much.

I was displaying, I was told, the classic symptoms of a "benevolent sexist." In other words, I was treating someone with excessive courtesy just to show that I was really in charge.

It's an idea that hasn't gone away. A recent issue of *Psychology of Women Quarterly* published a report showing that everyday acts that imply women should be cherished and protected are actually sinister forms of patriarchal control.

Offering to carry a woman's shopping bags to her car? You're implying she's weak.

Volunteering to walk a colleague to her car after dark? You're suggesting she's incapable of looking after her own safety.

Complimenting a woman on her cooking? You're reinforcing the old chestnut that a woman's place is in the kitchen.

Stopping to help a female motorist with a flat tire? You're insinuating that she is congenitally clueless about mechanical problems.

Huh. Let me just say that if anybody ever sees me standing at the side of the road beside a baffed-out car, feel free to pull over and give me a hand. I don't know a tire iron from a windshield wiper, so I'll be grateful for any help I can get—and I don't care if you're wearing mechanic's overalls or a miniskirt.

Cooking? I can burn water. Anybody of any gender who offers me a home-cooked meal can expect to be slobbered on effusively. You want to carry out my groceries? Sure. I've done that—it's tiring. Fill your boots. If it's after dark and a dodgy part of town I'll be happy to walk you to your car. It's not that I'm a Kung Fu expert or even an NHL defenceman, but I'm big and ugly enough to qualify as masher repellent. It's been so long since anybody hit on me I can't even remember which one wears the dog collar.

As for holding open doors, I still do that—for everybody, male or female.

So sue me.

Mind you, I'm careful not to say anything while I'm holding the door. I am mindful of the time Clare Booth Luce collided with her rival, Dorothy Parker, in a doorway. Ms. Luce stepped to one side and hissed "Age before beauty."

Sweeping through the doorway, Parker purred over her shoulder, "Pearls before swine."

Peanut Farmers
and Guinea Worms

*Celebrities in general are chosen, like the Calendar of
Saints, to meet certain needs: thus Frank Sinatra is the
patron celebrity of comebacks, Liza Minnelli of daughters,
and Jackie Onassis of curious marriages.*

—WILFRID SHEED

And what of another celebrity from that era? What of James Earl
Carter, thirty-ninth president of the United States? What's he the
patron saint of?

Republican one-liners, mostly. Jimmy Carter had the misfortune to
serve during a sluggish patch for the US economy. He wasn't the cause
but he carried the can for it. Mr. Carter also lacked the hard-nosed, lick-
'em-in-the-alley posture American voters seem to favour in their presi-
dents. He didn't strut and boast like George W., lacked the matinee idol
profile of Reagan, wasn't slick like Clinton or wily like Nixon.

He was also responsible for some highly questionable decisions in
foreign affairs. He gave the Panama Canal back to the Panamanians for
gawd's sake! And he wasted a lot of time and energy over pansy issues
like world peace and the eradication of disease in developing nations.
American voters rewarded Carter by booting him out of office in 1981
and handing his opponent, Ronald Reagan, a forty-four-state landslide.

But celebrityhood lasts a lifetime, if not longer, and being a failure as
president is no liability to the bank account. Richard Nixon was an Oval
Office disgrace but he subsequently got $600,000 for two interviews

with David Frost and $2.3 million for his memoirs. Gerald Ford, the man Lyndon Johnson said "couldn't chew gum and walk at the same time," earned a post-presidential income of over $1 million a year.

Even George W., who left his country's economy in smoking ruins while earning an approval rating of 22 percent, still manages to find audiences willing to hear him mispronounce some speechwriter's platitudes at 150 grand a pop.

Jimmy Carter didn't go on the celebrity speakers' circuit when he left the Oval Office. Instead, he donned a carpenter's apron and (more derisive snickers from the Tuskers on the US right) went out to help build affordable houses on behalf of Habitat for Humanity.

He also continued his fight against diseases endemic to emerging nations. Diseases like AIDS, dengue fever, malaria and a particularly nasty little bastard called the Guinea worm.

It is a pestilence that has been with us for thousands of years. The Bible refers to the creature as "the fiery serpent." Guinea worms are rather snakelike—they can grow to a metre in length. Their preferred hangout: inside your body.

Or rather, inside the bodies of the desperately poor in countries like Ethiopia, Mali, Ghana and Sudan. The modus operandi of the Guinea worm reads like a plot summary for a Stephen King novel. It hatches in ponds, enters a victim's body, usually through a cut or scratch, then proceeds to grow. In its mature stage when the Guinea worm is as long as a man's belt, it gnaws a hole through the skin and sticks its head out, looking for more water than it can find in its host. This is when the Guinea worm can be removed. Slowly, excruciatingly, millimetres at a time, by laboriously winding the emerged portion around a stick. The pain, I am told, is breathtaking.

You don't ever want to make the acquaintance of the Guinea worm—bad enough to see them infesting someone else. In places like Sudan, victims can have up to a dozen of the creatures dangling from their bodies, a sight one imagines Jimmy Carter has seen all too frequently. In 1986 as part of his post-presidential career he established the Carter Center to lead a global battle against the epidemic. At that time nearly four million people in twenty countries carried the Guinea worm. Today, there are just 3,200 known cases worldwide, mostly in Sudan. The solution is simple and decidedly low-tech. Find the victims, move them into compounds to feed and treat them and provide them with clean water to keep them away from ponds. Hostless, the Guinea worms are left to starve. Experts predict that in two more years the disease will be officially extinct.

That's what Jimmy Carter's living for these days. He's pushing ninety now, still ensconced on his famous peanut farm in Plains, Georgia. Asked by a reporter if he had any unfinished goals in life, Carter replied, "to outlive the Guinea worm."

Then he laughed and added, "All I have to do is live two more years and I'll achieve my goal."

Quite a legacy: President of the USA, recipient of the Nobel Peace Prize, conqueror of the Guinea worm.

And my nomination for Patron Saint of Decency.

Those Revolting Animals

Whoever first floated the concept of "dumb animals" was, well, dumb. Sure, they probably meant "dumb" as in "speechless." That's even dumber. Cows moo, sheep bleat, crows caw and lions roar. Pigeons, Pomeranians, puff adders and porpoises coo, yap, hiss and squeak respectively. The fact that humans can't speak their languages doesn't make them speechless.

As for evidence of intelligence, how about a candidate that raises armies for war, builds bridges and vast labyrinths, keeps slaves, raises herds for milking and employs chemical warfare to defeat its enemies? That would be the ant—which also employs child labour and attacks all trespassers on sight. (They're social creatures but they ain't NDP.)

Nope, animals are neither voiceless nor stupid—and there's evidence that they're getting a little fed up with the awkward hairless bipeds who've had the audacity to claim dominion over them for the past few millennia.

Put more simply: Heads up. The animals are revolting.

Strictly anecdotal evidence so far—a random incident here and there. Like the one that befell Jerry Barnes and his sailboat off the coast of Oregon recently. There was Jerry, tootling along to an offshore race, minding his jibs and halyards when suddenly about a metre off the port bow something very like a slimy railroad car rose out of the water, kept rising, thirty feet, forty feet, then turned and fell.

On Jerry Barnes' sailboat.

"Holy @#%$&+!" remarked a member of the crew, eloquently.

The rigging was fouled, the mast was snapped in three pieces and the boat was disabled enough to require a tow back to shore. The whale—a humpback, they think—swam away. No one on board was hurt but the cetacean's point was emphatically made: get the hell out of my backyard.

Then there was the guy who got knifed by a chicken down in California. Jose Luis Ochoa, age thirty-five, was attending an illegal backwoods cockfight, got a little too close to the action and got stabbed in the calf by the knife/spur of one of the fighting roosters. It wasn't Jose's day. A cop raid followed; Jose took off and bled to death while hiding in the woods.

Not that humans are going down without a fight. Erin Sullivan proved that recently by his encounter with a police dog in Glendale, Arizona. Sullivan was burgling a Glendale home when he was interrupted on the job by a four-legged member of the Glendale police department. The dog bit Sullivan. Sullivan bit the dog. Now Sullivan is suing the police department for "interfering with his civil rights." The fact that Sullivan filed his lawsuit from a prison where he's serving eight years for the Glendale burglary does not enhance his chances.

But when it comes to the animal world one should never be too quick to judge. Witness the case of David Bowering of Toronto. Bowering spent six months working as a CUSO volunteer in Kenya back in the 1960s. One day during his stay he came upon a young bull elephant standing apart from the herd, one front leg raised awkwardly in the air. The animal was clearly distressed.

Bowering approached and carefully knelt down before the beast. He could see a large, jagged splinter embedded in the bottom of the elephant's foot. With infinite patience Bowering opened his pocketknife and gingerly worked the splinter out. The elephant put its foot down on the ground and stared at Bowering for what seemed an eternity. Bowering didn't move—frozen to the spot. He knew he could easily get trampled into a stain on the African jungle floor.

Instead, the elephant lifted its trunk almost in a salute and slowly walked into the bush. Bowering learned not to talk about the encounter. No one believed him.

Forty-five years later a retired David Bowering was walking through the Metropolitan Toronto Zoo with a group of colleagues. When they approached the elephant enclosure, one of the older bulls seemed to be looking at him. "He likes you, Dave," a friend remarked. Slowly the elephant detached himself from the herd and came over to face

Bowering at the railing. The old bull stared, then slowly lifted its front left foot. Up, down, up, down, up, down—three times, never taking his eyes off Bowering.

Could this be the same elephant he'd helped in Kenya all those years ago? On a hunch, Bowering climbed over the enclosure, walked up to the elephant and stared into its eye. The bull elephant trumpeted loudly, wrapped its trunk around Bowering and slammed him into the railing, killing him instantly.

Probably wasn't the same elephant.

Baby, It's Gold Outside

A long time ago when pterodactyls flew and I first entered the job market I found myself one payday with some spare cash in my bank account. "Invest it!" whispered my Good Fairy. "In what?" I asked. "Gold!" whispered GF.

I had, that payday, enough money in my account to buy twenty ounces of the yellow stuff but I took a pass. Other pleasures beckoned seductively—a down payment on a decent used car, a Caribbean vacation, a couple of scalped front row tickets to a Rolling Stones concert. Besides, the price of gold was ridiculously high.

Thirty-five dollars an ounce.

What's that old German saying: "Too soon old; too late smart"? If I'd bought those twenty ounces of gold back then it would be a pretty rosy nest egg to slip under the mattress right now. The price of gold is still streaking skyward as I type. That's mighty pricey for a cold, hard substance that you can't eat, drink or make love to, but gold has mesmerized humankind for as long as we've been winkling it out of the earth. And that's a long time. Archeologists have uncovered golden artefacts in the Balkans that date back to 4,000 BC. The earliest known map ever found includes plans for a gold mine in the Nubian Desert. The Egyptians literally worshipped the stuff. Romans commandeered legions of slaves to dig for it. The Aztecs called it (presumably with admiration) *teocuitlatl*, which means "God's excrement."

So what's the big attraction? Well, gold is beautiful, it doesn't rust and although it's dense, gold is extremely workable. In fact, it's the most malleable of all the metals. A single ounce of gold could be beaten into a sheet 300 feet square. Gold leaf can be beaten so thin you can read a newspaper through it.

The other thing that makes gold attractive is, it's hard to come by. Acquisitive humans have been prospecting, pick-axing, panning and smelting for gold for 6,000 years, and yet all the gold that's ever been found would amount to 180 thousand tons, give or take an earring. That would fit into a cube just twenty-five yards high, wide and deep.

Gold fever runs like a recurrent plague through the pages of history. The conquistadores slaughtered for it in Central and South America. Forty-niners and Klondikers gave up their jobs and families to chase traces of the stuff in streams from California to the Yukon.

And the fever is upon us again—which is not necessarily a good sign. Henry Jarecki, a famous dealer in gold bullion says, "The world is a pleasanter place when there are low gold prices. Low prices signify trust and friendship."

Both of which are in apparently short supply these days. JP Morgan recently announced that it had reopened its gold vault beneath the streets of New York. The vault has been closed for years, but the investment bank obviously anticipates a bout of gold fever for some time to come. They are also building a brand new gold vault beneath the streets of Singapore.

Canada's in on the act too. Not far from JP Morgan headquarters in New York—at 26 Broadway to be precise—our own Bank of Nova Scotia maintains a massive gold vault. Here at home the folks at BNS would be happy to sell you a gold bar or wafer—anything from one to four hundred ounces worth, for just a slight extra charge over the going price.

Good investment? Most financial advisors think not. They point out that gold prices are volatile and extremely sensitive to outside forces as unpredictable as hurricanes and threats of war (or peace).

Yet history shows us that people of all times and cultures draw comfort from the hoarding of gold.

All I know is, if I'd taken the plunge all those years ago and bought a few ounces of gold I'd be sitting pretty right now. Not that I'm hurting, you understand. I've got all the money I'll ever need.

As long as I don't buy anything.

Come to think of it, back when I had that chance to buy gold at $35 an ounce, a cup of coffee was selling for a dime. This morning I bought a cup of Grandioso Machiavelli Frappalatte something-or-other at Starbucks. It's lukewarm, smells like coffee and set me back six bucks and change.

To hell with precious metals. If I'd been smart enough to invest in coffee bean futures I'd be drinking out of a golden goblet instead of a cardboard cup.

Gender Blending

My nomination for most politically incorrect song title of all time: The showstopper from the musical *My Fair Lady* entitled "Why Can't a Woman Be More like a Man?"

Sure, it's a fifty-five-year-old chestnut that was written tongue-in-cheek and actually takes the mickey out of macho, but tongue-in-cheek doesn't play well in these earnest times. Taken at face value the title is provocatively incendiary; it's calculated to set Maidenforms a-smoulder at a hundred paces.

Gender equality has been a dicey business ever since Adam and Eve elected to turn over a new leaf. Then we had Jack and Jill mobilizing that bucket brigade ascent to the well on the hill, ostensibly in search of water. You'll recall that it didn't end well—Jill took a bad tumble and Jack ended up with a possible concussion and whiplash—but at least the damage was gender neutral.

Which I guess is what the folks in charge of that preschool in Sweden are aiming for. The administrators at Egalia Preschool near Stockholm have initiated a policy to "avoid instilling gender stereotypes in our students." Accordingly, kiddies at the school wear identical, shapeless blue vests. The boys are encouraged to play with kitchen utensils; the girls are urged to get down and dirty with the toy trucks and tractors.

"Society expects girls to be girlie, nice and pretty and boys to be manly, rough and outgoing," says Jenny Johnsson, a thirty-one-year-old teacher. "Egalia gives them a fantastic opportunity to be whoever they want to be."

Which is fair enough I guess, given that Walmart has announced plans to market a full line of makeup including mascara, sheer lip gloss, pink blush and purple eye shadow—aimed at eight-year-old children.

You read right—eight-year-olds.

People fight the marketing machine any way they can. It's not surprising that a Toronto couple became a publicity sensation recently—not so much because they named their new baby Storm, but because they declined to announce whether Storm was a boy or a girl. The father declared that he found it obnoxious to identify a child's gender on the basis of his/her/its genitalia. "If you really want to get to know someone," said David Stocker, "you don't ask what's between their legs." Then mom and dad announced that their child's gender would be revealed "only when Storm decides Storm would like to share."

Predictably, the world went nuts. Columnists sneered and editorialists tut-tutted. The parents were deluged, denounced and roundly proselytized upon. Cynics were absolutely certain it was an attention-getting media con à la Octomom or the boy in the supposedly runaway weather balloon.

Not true. In a letter to the editor of the *Ottawa Citizen,* Storm's mother, Kathy, explained:

"The strong, lightning-fast, vitriolic response was a shock . . . To protect our children from the media frenzy we did not anticipate, we have declined over 100 requests for interviews from all over the world, including offers to fly to New York all expenses paid and to appear on almost every American morning show. We have learning to do, parks to visit and butterflies to care for."

We've been down this gender bender road before. Almost three centuries ago, as a matter of fact. Let me introduce you to a pair of the blood-thirstiest pirates ever to sail the waters of the Caribbean. One was a nasty piece of work named Read; the other was a savage, tattooed brute who answered to Bonny. In 1721 a Jamaican warship cornered their pirate galleon and a bloody battle ensued. The pirates were finally defeated. Read and Bonny were the last to drop their cutlasses.

British justice was swift and final. The entire pirate crew was tried, pronounced guilty and hanged.

Except for Read and Bonny, who were spared.

They were pregnant, you see. Bonny's first name was Anne; Read's was Mary.

That's the thing about gender stereotypes. They have a tendency to turn around and bite you.

Right in the assumption.

Germ Warfare

There's a photograph on my living room wall that was taken by a neighbour, of a neighbour. It's a head-and-shoulders close-up portrait of Malcolm, our local, among other things, veterinarian. Malcolm is also a farmer and the photograph was taken just after he'd come in from a morning working in the fields. We call it "The Potato Digger" and it is a remarkable portrait. Malcolm looks wise and weary and weathered.

But it's his hand that gets me.

He's rubbing his chin with his right hand and the fingers, knuckles and nails of that hand are bemired, begrimed and utterly muckified. They are dirty. Magnificently, triumphantly, unequivocally dirty.

Well, what do you expect? The man's been digging up potatoes.

You can infer a great deal about Malcolm from that photograph, but one thing you know for a certainty: the man is not a mysophobe.

Mysophobe? A twenty-five cent word for germ freak. Mysophobes suffer an intense fear of dirt and contamination, often washing their hands, clothes and surroundings obsessively. Howie Mandel is one. The comedian will not shake hands with anyone unless he's wearing latex gloves. (As host of the TV show *Deal or No Deal*, however, he has been known to fist bump, bear hug and even kiss the better-looking contestants—proving that just because you're a neurotic doesn't mean you're smart.)

Another Howie—mega-tycoon and certified nutbar Howard Hughes—was a five-star mysophobe. He wouldn't handle money and ordered that his used bedsheets be burned, not washed. If he wanted to read a magazine Hughes had his flunkies buy three copies and deliver them on a cart. He would select the middle issue without touching the other two, which were subsequently burned. He also had a charming way of dealing with doorknobs. He simply kicked the door, a signal for a staff member to open it.

Most mysophobes aren't that far gone; they're just a teensy bit paranoid about germs. And, not to go all paranoid or anything, but . . . could I just put a handkerchief over my mouth and whisper this in your ear?

I think mysophobes are taking over the planet.

Increasingly when I enter a store in a shopping mall the first thing I bump into is a hand sanitizer dispensing station where I am cheerily invited to spritz myself free of contamination. My local supermarket features tubs of free disinfectant swabs just outside the buggy corral so I can wipe down the handle of my shopping cart.

And I don't know how it is at your health provider's office but if you plan to spend any time in my hospital waiting room, best bring along your bedside copy of *War and Peace*. Those familiar, dog-eared copies of *Maclean's* and *Chatelaine* from 1987 have finally been tossed out. Germs, don't you know.

Public rest rooms? Hah. Any mysophobe can tell you that you'd have to be a suicidal fool to walk within a hundred feet of a public rest room these days. Those places are microbial maternity wards. Festering hives of fetid effluvia toxic enough to turn an innocent human into a gibbering radioactive mutant.

Diabolical, too. Sure, they offer sinks to wash your hands after using the facilities but you have to use your hand to turn the tap on and off, right? Just like umpteen-dozen feces-laden hands before you—and you still have to open the door to get out of the place.

Where's a Howard Hughes flunky when you need him?

Makes you wonder how mankind managed to muddle through the past couple of hundred thousand years, often without so much as a surgical mask or a packet of Handi Wipes.

Hundreds of anti-bacterial products crowd the shelves of our drug stores and supermarkets and, as medical experts keep trying to tell us, they're at best a waste of money, at worst hazardous to our health. Dr. Stuart Levy, director of Genetics and Drug Resistance at Tufts University in Boston says such products upset the natural balance of microorganisms in our systems. "Bacteria are a natural, and needed, part of life," he says. "Most live blamelessly. In fact, they often protect us from disease because they compete with, and thus limit the proliferation of, pathogenic bacteria."

A little dirt is good for us. Dr. Levy knows it. My veterinarian knows it. So do you and I.

Howard Hughes? He may have been a billionaire genius, but he never managed to figure that out.

Money Can't Buy You Love

I have the feeling that in a balanced life one should die penniless. The trick is in dismantling.

—ART GARFUNKEL

Ah, yes: money. Tricky commodity, that. Money—more specifically the pursuit of it—has besmirched and bedevilled humankind since . . . forever. Since the first Neanderthal con artist turned to his cavemate and grunted the equivalent of "Sweet loincloth. I'll give you thirty clamshells for it."

Cash, bread, scratch, dough, long green, filthy lucre. Money has assumed many names and many forms over the eons—from cowrie shells in China to whale teeth in Fiji. The ancient Aztecs used chocolate (cacao seeds) as currency. Other cultures have favoured everything from ivory to livestock, arrowheads to spices, tobacco to wampum.

It was always all about money as, alas, it still so often is. The writer James Baldwin, who spent a lot of years without much of it, concluded that money was exactly like sex. "You thought of nothing else if you didn't have it," wrote Baldwin, "and thought of other things if you did."

A newspaper reporter once asked a famous holdup artist named Willie Sutton why he robbed so many banks. Sutton regarded the reporter as if he was perhaps a little slow and replied gently, "Because that's where the money is."

Well, duh.

Money. It shapes our lives; some would say it warps them. Unless we refuse to play, like Karl Rabeder did. Herr Rabeder, an Austrian aged forty-seven, used to swim in the deep end of the money pool. He lived in a villa in the Austrian Alps and vacationed in a nineteenth-century farmhouse in Provence, all thanks to a thriving international furniture business that left him with a fortune of $5 million in the bank.

And then one day he decided he would give it all away. Sold the villa, the chateau and the business, set up charities in Central and South America and endowed them with his fortune—every cent.

"Money is counterproductive," he told a reporter for the *Daily Telegraph*. "It prevents happiness to come." Rabeder says he plans to retreat to a small wooden shack in the mountains. His friends and family? They think he's nuts—they told him so. He's not listening to them. "I was just listening," he says, "to the voice of my heart and soul."

Good luck to Mr. Rabeder—but I bet if James Baldwin was still around he'd be rolling his eyes. It's easy to be philosophical about money when you have a garage full of it; less so when you're a bit short. Money is like any addictive drug: the less you have in your system, the more powerful it is.

And yet what are we talking about? Not ivory, not gold or silver—not even loincloths. We're talking about wrinkly bits of paper festooned with numbers and symbols in coloured ink. A hundred-dollar bill buys a hundred dollars worth of goods and/or services only because you and I and the bank manager believe it does. Paper money is an act of faith. Ask any German who lived through the 1930s, when it took a wheelbarrow full of Deutschemarks to buy a loaf of bread. Ask anybody in Zimbabwe, where last I heard, the annual inflation rate had topped 231 million percent.

Ask Dominik Podolsky what paper money is good for. Mr. Podolsky, a snowboarder from Munich, was stranded on a mountainside in the Alps overnight. He kept warm by crinkling up all the paper money he had in his pockets and setting fire to it.

Reminds me of the story of the London gent making use of one of the stalls in a public lavatory who realizes—too late—that his particular stall is sporting only an empty cardboard roll where the toilet paper should be. Fortunately, he hears someone enter the stall next to his.

"I say, old chap," he calls out, "I seem to have run out of toilet paper. Would you be kind enough to pass some under the partition?"

"Sorry, mate," says the voice next door. "Doesn't seem to be any in here either."

"Oh," says the gent. "Then by any chance would you have two fives for a ten?"

The Emperor's Slip is Showing

Did you catch that photo in the newspapers of Vladimir Putin emerging from the Black Sea looking like James Bond, carrying two ancient Greek amphorae? Now, THAT'S the kind of photo op any politician would eat his left arm to be able to post on his website. What a coup! How prescient of the Russian president to have brought along government photographers on his vacation to record his moment of triumph—and on only his third time scuba diving! Gosh, many archeologists spend their whole careers dreaming of making a discovery like that. Pretty impressive.

And utterly bogus.

Somebody spilled the borscht on Putin's attempt at public relations. Turns out the 2,000-year-old jugs he "discovered" had actually been found during a legitimate archeological dig and conveniently placed off shore in a couple of metres of water. Putin didn't even need a wetsuit. All he had to do was bend down, stick his fingers in the handles, stand up and smile for the cameras.

I wonder how you say "hubris" in Russian?

The word comes from the same place those waterlogged amphorae did—ancient Greece. It's derived from the word *hybris*, which means, "wanton presumption toward the gods." Your grandmother would have called it being "too big for your britches." There's a lot of it going around. Has been for a long time.

Back in 1812 the Emperor of France, King of Italy and master of continental Europe, one Napoleon Bonaparte, decided he was ready to take on Russia. He assembled an army of 500,000 soldiers and despite the urgent warnings of his top officers and advisors started marching on Moscow. Later that same year in the dead of winter barely 20,000 frostbitten and emaciated French survivors staggered back to France.

Hubris one; Bonaparte, no score.

The late and unlamented Moammar Gadhafi spent his last forty years wrapped in the coils of hubris. He adored being photographed in buffoonish comic opera costumes, surrounded by a phalanx of big-bosomed Amazonian bodyguards. He ended up, as the world knows, being hauled squealing out of a drainage pipe in the desert.

Mussolini with his chest puffed out like a pouter pigeon; Hitler with his lunatic, rabid dog stare; Mao bobbing like a bloated cork in the Yangtze (BELOVED LEADER SWIMS 15 KM IN 65 MINUTES, the Chinese press gushed). What is it about the siren song of front-page glory that tempts leaders to look so ridiculous so often?

Western leaders are not immune to the disease of hubris. George (the Dim One) Bush will live on in history, if only for the incredibly tone-deaf photograph that shows him grinning, duded up like a for-real fighter pilot on the deck of an aircraft carrier with a banner reading "Mission Accomplished" behind him. The year was 2003. One hundred and thirty-nine American casualties had been recorded in Iraq. In less than a decade another four thousand US troops would die there—not to mention (as they almost never are) hundreds of thousands of Iraqi civilians. Bush's oblivious cowboy cockiness makes the photograph appear even hollower.

And Canadian leaders? That brings us to Lake Okanagan and a press conference in the year 2000. Stockwell Day is running hard for the prime minister's office. Actually, he's riding hard—full throttle—on a Jet Ski, wearing a skin-tight wetsuit. He looks très buff—especially for a Canadian politician. He slews the Jet Ski up to the dock, flashes a 500-kilowatt Hollywood grin and indicates to reporters that he's ready to take questions.

It should have worked. Instead the members of the Fourth Estate all but wet their pants laughing. Instantly, Stockwell Day became the butt of ten thousand jokes from coast to coast to coast. Somebody should have warned him that Canadians don't do hubris so well.

And from all appearances neither do the Irish. Back in October they elected Michael D. Higgins as their president. At age seventy, short and bald, he's an unlikely candidate for PR photos riding on a

Jet Ski, swaggering on a flight deck or hoisting Greek amphorae out of the ocean. Mr. Higgins, a poet, a politician and a peace activist, was described in the *Irish Times* as "avuncular, erudite, experienced with the Irish gift for language and tune, a bockety knee and a whiff of diddly-aye for the Yanks."

I don't care how he'd look in a wet suit; if I was Irish he'd have my vote.

Up, Up and A-Weigh

*For the first time ever, overweight people outnumber
the average people in America. Doesn't that make
"overweight" the "average," then? Last month you were
fat, now you're average—hey, let's get a pizza!*

—Jay Leno

T'ain't funny, McGee. According to the World Health Organization, the US is now officially the world's third-chubbiest nation. Nearly 70 percent of Americans are packing serious excess poundage. They follow American Samoa and Kiribati, two tiny island nations in the South Pacific where natives have embraced imported American crap food so enthusiastically that their three major food groups appear to be cheeseburgers, beer and Spam. Canada? You'll feel smug to know that we don't even make the top ten, but we're not that far behind. According to WHO few human beings this side of Somalia, are. WHO statisticians claim that one in three of the world's adults is overweight and that one in ten is flat-out obese.

That works out to 1.6 billion bulgy bipeds, worldwide—slightly more than the entire population of China. WHO predicts that number will balloon by an astonishing 40 percent in just the next ten years.

Why the obesity epidemic? Pretty simple: calories in, calories out. I live on an island. The Irish immigrants who settled this land just a few generations ago thought nothing of rowing five miles to the end of the bay every Sunday then walking another five miles to a church for a three-hour service. And when that was over they got to do the trip in reverse—clad all the while in their hot and woolly Sunday best.

I spend most of my waking hours sitting in front of a computer or splayed on a sofa reading a book or driving, not walking, to various destinations. What's more, my forbears fuelled themselves with real food, not processed puke from the Kwik-E-Mart or the Shop 'n Save Grosseteria. On the way home from church I'm pretty sure they hardly ever stopped for a double dip Rocky Roads in a waffle cone.

I'm not pointing fingers here. My physical profile is hardly Brandoesque but it ain't exactly elfin either. Like just about everybody else I know I could stand to lose a few pounds.

But it's not easy. Do you know what's in just about every morsel of processed food that you put in your mouth? Corn syrup. Know what it's good for? Almost nothing—aside from making you fatter.

On the other hand I can offer my fellow blimps one small consolation—we're better in the sack. That's not my fantasy—it's the conclusion of a Turkish university study released just last month. The year-long project correlated body mass index with male sexual performance. It found that men with significant excess body fat "last longer" when it comes to making love than their slimmer counterparts.

Before we start winking lewdly and high-fiving each other you should know the reason. It's female hormones. Fat guys appear to have more of a female sex hormone called estradiol than skinny guys do. The experts reckon this extra chemical baggage slows down a tubby chap's sexual response mechanism, making him less "flash in the pan," if you catch my drift.

Maybe—but I'm not buying it. I don't have any university studies to back me up, but I'd wager a tofu and bean sprouts stir-fry against a bushel basket of Chicken McNuggets that romantically speaking a lanky lad like Brad Pitt hits more homers than Fat Albert.

As for food advice, I guess you could do worse than the seven-word mantra from Michael Pollan, the American journalist, who advised, "Eat food. Not too much. Mostly plants."

I also like the advice from the comedian Lewis Black, who recommends his favourite health club—the International House of Pancakes: "Because no matter what you weigh, there will always be somebody who weighs a hundred and fifty pounds more than you."

My personal tip for you: When standing on the bathroom scales, always remember to hold your stomach in.

You'll still weigh the same, but you'll be able to see the numbers.

Old Age—Thinking Outside the Box

Getting old ain't for pussies.

—ANON

Indeed it ain't. Getting old is a curious journey—the trail signs are sometimes confusing and hard to read and the stations aren't well marked. I never realized I was "getting on" until people started telling me how good I looked. Nobody commented on my vitality when I was seventeen, twenty-five or even forty-five, but now that I'm a greybeard, the air is full of "Hey, you're looking great!" and "Wow! Did you lose some weight?"

I'm pretty sure what they mean is: "Hmm, I see you're not dead yet."

You bet I'm not. And I've got no plans to "go gentle" either. I've long admired the poem Dylan Thomas wrote for his dying father—and especially his advice to "rage, rage, against the dying of the light."

Not that the Welshman knew what he was talking about.

Dylan Thomas boozed his way into oblivion long before he became eligible to receive his old age pension. The man's last words before he passed out in a heap on the floor of a New York City gin joint were: "I've had eighteen straight whiskies. I believe that's a record."

Dylan Thomas was just thirty-nine, still decades away from any first-hand knowledge of the dirty tricks advancing age dispenses—the stiff joints, the bad sleeps, the, as Leonard Cohen put it, "aches in the places where I used to play."

I believe there's another well-known consequence of aging but I can't recall it offhand.

But I do recall a report from the Canadian Institute for Health Information that came out last month. It indicates almost half—45 percent—of residents in nursing homes and similar residences show symptoms of depression.

Imagine that. You take old folks out of their homes, away from their families, their pets, their routines and ensconce them in unfamiliar surroundings among strangers and caregivers serving institutional food prepared by other strangers—and they tend to get a little down in the mouth. Who could possibly have foreseen that?

What's worse according to the report is that the depressive symptoms are frequently undiagnosed and hence left untreated.

It doesn't have to be that way. Dr. Marie-France Rivard, an Ottawa psychiatrist who specializes in geriatrics, says it's crucial to get our elders' caregivers onside because "depression is a very treatable illness and with appropriate identification and treatment, the quality of life of people can be much improved."

Of course one must always be alert to the danger of too much attentiveness. Take my pal Steve. He's a well-respected elder with lots of good friends but alas, no living family. He finally got a little too old and frail to look after his farm so he sold it and moved into an extended care facility.

And it's a high-end joint. The rooms are warm and roomy, the food is great and the staff is incredibly helpful and devoted. On his first day there a nurse sat Steve on his bed and began to explain the facilities. As she talked she noticed that Steve was slowly beginning to list to one side. The nurse sprang up and gently pushed him upright. As she was leaving the room she happened to look back and there was Steve, sitting on the bed but definitely teetering to starboard again. She rushed back and straightened him up. Just to be on the safe side she called a nurse's aide and asked her to stay with Steve in case he started to fall over once more.

Sure enough, five times Steve started to lean; five times the nurse's aide got him vertical again.

I went in to visit Steve that night and asked him how he liked the place.

"It's not too bad," Steve allowed, "except they won't let you fart."

Save the Salmon

That Saturday afternoon the Victoria weather was BC perfect. Blue sky, hot sun, cool breeze. Perfect for a round of golf, a trip to the beach, a hike in the bush . . . or a salmon migration through the streets washing up at the headwaters of the BC Legislature. More than five thousand BCers chose to do the migration. There were Native elders in traditional robes and headdresses cheek by jowl with skateboarders in elbow pads and helmets. There were moms pushing strollers, oldsters with canes, school kids, street people, ecofreaks, farmers, fisherfolk, tourism operators, Oak Bay tweedies, James Bay yuppies—even the odd politician, though none representing the clan Campbell. No one there to represent the fish farms either. The 100 percent Norwegian-owned fish farms that dot our salmon migration routes. A pity because the demonstration was aimed at those two entities, government and corporate.

The marchers had a simple message. They scrawled it on placards, they beat it out on drums and they chanted it in slogans but it really came down to just two words: Get. Out.

Get your farmed fish operations out of the West Coast waterways where the sea lice they generate are threatening the survival of BC's wild salmon. Get Out.

Who says so? Alexandra Morton does. She is the silver-haired Boadicea of the save the salmon movement. Is she right? I don't know. I'm not a marine biologist—like Alexandra Morton. I haven't spent my career in the Broughton Archipelago studying the habits of wild salmon—like Alexandra Morton. And I'm not tough enough to slug it out for twenty years with hostile fish farmers and oblivious politicos—like Alexandra Morton.

And I'm sure as hell not rugged enough to walk 500 kilometres down the length of Vancouver Island to fetch up at the BC Leg shouting "Wake up in there!"—like Alexandra Morton.

A lot of smart people think she's right. Vicky Husband, Order of BC, Order of Canada, West Coast chair of the Sierra Club, sang Alexandra's praises. Rafe Mair, ex-cabinet minister and BC's most famous radio broadcaster, did the same.

These days Rafe can barely walk unaided, but he can still roar like the MGM lion. He blistered the stone walls of the BC Legislature with his disdain for the government's mishandling of our wild salmon. Then Stuart Phillip spoke. The grand chief of the Union of BC Indian Chiefs does not roar but he radiates grace. He bestowed upon Alexandra Morton the highest honour his people can confer: a cedar headband with a single eagle feather.

Billy Proctor spoke too. Billy is the quintessence of the BC West Coast white male spirit. Born in the Broughton Archipelago seventy-four years ago. Logger, builder, mechanic, salmon hatcher and most especially a fisherman for more than half a century, Billy is lean and wiry and weathered.

He's got mighty, meaty hands like baseball mitts, all scarred and lumpy and, well, worked, from decades of handling nets and gaffs and fish hooks and fish knives.

He told the crowd on the legislature lawn about one river in the Broughton Archipelago where just fifteen years ago runs of 300,000 pinks a year were common. Last year government experts checked the river. They found fewer than 200 fish. Billy Proctor doesn't shout or chant. He says his piece quietly: Those Norwegian fish farms, he says, are killing our wild salmon.

Alexandra Morton spoke at the end of the afternoon that Saturday. She looked tired but serene and she held up a token. It was the toothy jawbone of a chum salmon she'd plucked from a stream up in the Broughton and carried in her backpack all the way down to the bottom end of the island. At the end of her speech she placed it carefully on the steps of the BC Legislature. We can only hope that jawbone somehow magically leaps up and bites the appropriate politicians in the ass.

Still Nutsoid After All These Years

The two most abundant commodities in the universe are hydrogen and stupidity.

—HARLAN ELLISON

There is more stupidity than hydrogen in the universe, and it has a longer shelf life.

—FRANK ZAPPA

Vivienne and Knox could be forgiven for thinking they'd landed at Stupidity HQ. They came to earth a couple of summers back as twins born to Brad Pitt and Angelina Jolie. Their arrival was greeted with a $14 million inaugural nest egg lobbed in from deep right field. That's how much *People* magazine, in partnership with *Hello*, another dumbass tabloid, paid for the privilege of publishing the first, exclusive photos of the kids.

Fourteen million dollars for a one-time photo with a couple of newborns—pretty stupid alright. But such rags are devoted to sustaining the lush groves of celebrity egos that thrive in the Hollywood Hills and stupidity is the manure that nurtures celebrity. How else to explain the continuing fascination with patent airheads like Christina Aguilera ("So where's the Cannes Film Festival being held this year?"); Don King ("He speaks English and Spanish and he's bilingual too."); and Arnold Schwarzenegger ("I think gay marriage is something that should be between a man and a woman.")?

And if that's not bummer enough for you, consider this grim stat: as of this writing Britney Spears has more than four million followers on Twitter.

The irony is that we live in a supposedly sophisticated age. People have never had easier access to the accumulated wisdom of the ages. Our libraries, museums and art galleries are open to all. We have wall-to-wall radio, TV and smart phones. The latest information on everything from aardvarks to zyzzyva is available at the punch of a Google search button.

And yet . . . Sarah Palin.

We seem to be getting actually dumber.

That may not be an illusion. A University of Wisconsin anthropologist has analyzed human skulls collected from around the globe and spanning the past five millennia. His conclusion: the human brain is shrinking. According to John Hawks' data, human brains have shrivelled by about 150 cubic centimetres over the past 5,000 years. That's about 10 percent shrinkage of total brain mass.

Professor Hawks says that's not necessarily bad news; smaller brains don't have to be punier brains. It could be simply biological streamlining at work. "Maybe we got better with smaller brains," says Hawks—who then adds, unhelpfully: "But maybe we're getting dumber. How can we know?"

Thanks, professor.

Perhaps we can't nail down the human stupidity factor but we can certainly read the portentous crayon scrawls on the wall. Such as the fact that *Fox News*, featuring the spittle-flecked ravings of Bill O'Reilly and Sean Hannity (and, oh yes—Sarah Palin) reels in 2.6 million viewers on an average weeknight.

Still, put in perspective, that's not quite as scary as it sounds. Two and a half million viewers amounts to less than 1 percent of the American population—and we don't even get the service in most parts of Canada—or Canuckistan, as Bill the Loon likes to refer to us.

On the other hand—Andy Warhol. I note that a silkscreen of Andy's entitled *200 One-Dollar Bills* sold at public auction last fall at Sotheby's in New York. The painting is about eight-feet square and consists of a graphic representation of, er, one-dollar bills. Two hundred of them, side by side, marching across the canvas like a brick wall, only green.

It sold for $43.8 million USD.

Ah, well. Robertson Davies once said, "Every man is wise when attacked by a mad dog; fewer when pursued by a mad woman; only the wisest survive when attacked by a mad notion." I guess that goes for art collectors too.

And for the forces of officialdom, come to that. While attempting to board an aircraft in Newark, New Jersey, recently, Mikey Hicks was taken down by airport security. They were on to him right away because his name was on a suspected terrorist watch list.

Only problem was, the Newark Mikey Hicks was an eight-year-old Cub Scout from Clifton, N.J. His mother says he's been stopped, frisked, patted down and questioned at airports since he was two years old.

Crazy times. As Rita Mae Brown says, "One out of four people suffer from some form of nuttiness. Think of your three best friends. If they're okay, then it's you."

PART SIX

Did I Really Say That?

Be Careful What You Call Them

Canada's most famous philosopher Marshal McLuhan once observed that "the name of a man is a numbing blow from which he never recovers." I don't know for sure if that's true, but I do know that when it comes to names some men (and women) get hammered harder than others. Sir Reginald Aylmer Ranfurly Plunkett-Ernle-Erle-Drax comes to mind. He was (no kidding) an admiral in the British navy—though I daresay he never sailed a ship with an anchor heavier than the name he trailed behind him.

His friends just called him Reggie.

Alanis Morrisette's daughter won't be that lucky. The Ottawa-born songstress recently had a baby girl. Mom's announced that the child's name will be Ever Imre.

Ever. Imre. Let us try to calculate how many thousands of times that child will have to stop and explain her name to the curious.

"No, it's not 'Evelyn Marie,' it's 'Ever Imre.' No, not 'Emery'— 'Imre.' That's I-M-R-E . . . "

A numbing blow indeed. Names are tricky and volatile propositions. They're like lifelong licence plates and deserve considerable thought before they are bestowed. I remember the look on my mother's face when I told her that my daughter's middle name was going to be Gabrielle. Mom was a pioneer-stock, rock-ribbed Ontario Presbyterian—which is to say, plain spoken, no nonsense, no frills and definitely no fancy-pants names like Gabrielle. I might as well have told her we were naming the kid Jezebel or Nefertiti.

Mind you Mom was a polite Canuck, too, so she didn't say anything. Just blinked once or twice and started humming quietly.

Just as well she's gone to her reward these twenty years. If she had trouble handling Gabrielle how would she do with names like Acacia, Atlantis, Chevonne, Gulana and Quianne?

And that's just the first line of the local girls' hockey team.

Eco-consciousness looms large in the baby-naming game. There are kids answering to Sky, Rainbow, Snow, Spruce, Prairie and Leaf. But that's small potatoes compared to some of the Big Concept kids' names out there. Names like Freedom, Infinity, Horizon, Future and Diplomacy.

Only a matter of time before a skein of triplets named Surely, Goodness and Mercy shows up in the maternity ward.

Speaking of Surely, whatever happened to good old names like— well, Shirley? And Mary and Susan? And Tom, Dick and Harry? I guess nowadays parents just want their kids to stand out.

Which of course is the last thing most kids want to do.

Let us all thank our lucky stars that we were not born the off-spring of stars—which is to say, Hollywood celebrities. Celebs are the folks who really take it into the stratosphere when it comes to name-calling.

You think Alanis Morrisette's daughter's name is weird? Tell it to Frank Zappa's children—either his daughter Moon Unit or his son Dweezil. If that's still too tame for you, check out that potty-mouthed Vegas magician Penn Jillette. He called his daughter Moxie Crime Fighter. The actor Nicholas Cage was practically bland by comparison. He named his son Kal-El.

That's, uh, Superman's birth name back on Planet Krypton in case you didn't know.

No question weird names are weirdly hot right now but they are by no means an exclusively twenty-first-century phenomenon. Back in the last century when Sir Reginald Aylmer Ranfurly Plunkett-Ernle-Erle-Drax was stiff-upper-lipping his gin and tonics he had a contemporary named Sir William Walton. Sir William was a famous British composer by the time he died in 1983 but he had a bit of a scramble getting there. In his youth he was a typical starving artist who got by largely by scrounging off the goodwill of Dame Edith Sitwell. What he didn't know was the Sitwell family had a code name for Walton. They called him "Lincrusta."

Lincrusta was the trade name of an embossed wall covering made of gelled linseed oil and wood flour applied to heavy canvas.

It was known for being exceedingly difficult to peel off.

Caution, Guerrilla Poets Ahead

*Publishing a volume of verse is like dropping a rose petal
down the Grand Canyon and waiting for the echo.*

—Don Marquis

I can't remember exactly when I stopped reading poetry. Not in high school, for sure—I was mesmerized by Frost and Eliot, Pound and Dickinson. Not in my twenties either. Those years were saturated with the Beats and with Dylan. Not to mention a handsome young Montreal stud in a black leather jacket, name of Cohen.

Actually, I never lost my love of poetry—it was contemporary poetry that did me in. Nobody put it better than the American columnist Russell Baker who wrote: "I gave up on new poetry thirty years ago when most of it began to read like coded messages between lonely aliens in a hostile world."

Exactly. Somewhere toward the hind end of the twentieth century it seemed as if most poets turned their backs on the reading public in favour of playing increasingly obscure word games with each other. Poetry devolved into an exclusive ecosystem: poets writing for other poets, their editors, publishers and close blood relations. Readers can take a hint; they left in droves. Nowadays in most bookstores the Harry Potter shelf is longer than the entire poetry section. If there is a poetry section.

Which is a pity, because poetry matters. Ideally, it is as good as writing gets. Poetry is to prose, somebody once said, as dancing is to walking. The poet William Carlos Williams suggested that what passes for "the news" these days is a delusion. He said that the real news is in poems.

It is difficult
to get the news from poems
yet men die miserably every day
for lack
of what is found there.

But things have changed since the days when a Frost or a Sandberg or a Robert Service could fill a concert hall for a reading. Today, a poetry comeback would have to compete not just with the conventional print/radio/TV media, but also with the all-enveloping Internet—Facebook, YouTube—the entire Twitterverse.

Compete . . . or join in.

The good news is, a poet by the name of Elizabeth Bradfield may have found a way to re-inject poetry into the public bloodstream. For the past five years Bradfield has been stage-managing a phenomenon called Broadsided. It's a guerrilla project dedicated to, as its manifesto states, "putting literature and arts on the streets."

Bradfield's idea was to show people exactly why poetry matters—but first she had to get their attention. "I thought that perhaps if people ran into poetry on the streets, if poetry was paired with something eye-catching . . . then maybe I could persuade them that literature and art can speak to them directly and viscerally."

Here's how it works. Each month, Bradfield and a handful of editorial assistants choose a few poems from submissions emailed in by poetic hopefuls. Next, they invite graphic artists to "respond" to the poems with some original artwork. Bradfield and pals then marry the artwork with the poems and publish the results on the first of each month on their website as a "broadside"—a hoary term for a sheet of cheap paper printed on one side that nineteenth-century rabble rousers were wont to tack up around town to inform (or inflame) the public.

The next step is strictly twenty-first century. The poem/artwork goes on the website (www.broadsidedpress.org/) for all to see and use. Joe and Jane Poetrylover are free to download it, photocopy it and do whatever they like with the copies. The copied works show up on office bulletin boards, hospital waiting rooms, airplane seat pockets, even slipped into the pages of magazines and newspapers. "What subversive fun," says Bradfield, "to find poetry and art in a newspaper insert, when what you expect are ads for computer gear and cheap socks."

The world seems to agree. Bradfield's broadsides have been

published and dispersed on six continents and as far afield as Tasmania and Healy, Alaska.

Poetry running loose on the streets. What a concept. Marcus Valerius Martialus would understand. He's the Roman poet we call Martial and he wrote: "He does not write at all whose poems no man reads." Martial figured that out 1,900 years ago.

Seems like we're just catching up.

Hair Today, Gone Tomorrow

Guess what? They've just announced a cure for baldness! Seriously!!!! Researchers at the University of Pennsylvania School of Medicine have discovered that bald guys don't really lose their hair—it's merely "out of service." Their study claims all bald guys actually still have hair-generating stem cell embryos sleeping just under their scalps like so many dormant rhubarb bulbs. All those dozy cells need is a biologically induced wake-up call and hey, presto! Deserts bloom again. Luxuriant fulsome foliage where only shiny skin once reigned.

Of course, nobody's figured out exactly how to stimulate those stem cells yet, but as George Cotsarelis, the chief researcher told a reporter for *New Scientist* magazine: "This is pretty exciting and lowers the bar for (baldness) treatment."

Pretty exciting, indeed. Aren't you excited?

Nah, me neither.

As a career skinhead who hasn't carried a comb or fretted over dandruff for about thirty years, I'm okay with bald. Sure there's a slightly increased risk of frostbite and sunburn, but that's why they make Stetsons, Panamas, toques, fedoras, watch caps, derbys, berets, deerstalker hats and Thunder Bay Border Cats ball caps. And bald guys suit hats—unlike men with full heads of hair. When a hairy guy takes off his hat his head looks like the Liberty Bell.

As a matter of fact (and pardon me for baldly pointing it out) I am, when you get down to it, rather trendy. Three-quarters of the droopy-drawered multimillionaires who play in the National Basketball

Association shave their heads in an attempt to look as cool as me. Lots of football players, boxers and pro wrestlers ditch their head fur because a bald head makes them look, well, studlier. Tennis great Andre Agassi has less fuzz on his noggin than the balls he smashes over the net. And any hockey fans who think bald is wussy should try mentioning it to Mark Messier.

Hollywood embraced skinheads years ago. Back in the day a male lead with vacant acreage above his eyebrows was condemned to roles like country store grocer, machine shop union steward and small loan appraiser. Yul Brynner changed all that. He looked so good bald you didn't even want to think of him with hair. And after Brynner came Sean Connery, Samuel Jackson, Ben Kingsley, Telly Savalas and Stone Cold Steve Austin.

Okay . . . also Homer Simpson, William Shatner and Mini-Me. I never said bald was perfect.

I mentioned the new so-called cure for baldness to a sarcastic (and fulsomely thatched) pal down at the coffee shop. He smirked.

"Gimme a break," he said. "You know that if you could have a full head of hair tomorrow without surgery or drugs or a taxidermist, you'd jump at the chance."

Hmm. Would I? The answer is yes—on one condition. That I could have hair like Jeff Bridges. Have you seen him in a movie where he sports a full head of hair—like *The Fabulous Baker Boys* or *Crazy Heart*? The man looks like he's got a full-grown male African lion sitting on his head.

But of course my hair would not grow in like Jeff Bridges' hair does. I remember how my hair looked when I had it. My hair would grow in like a cross between Bride of Frankenstein and an abandoned heron's nest.

So my final answer to my sarcastic friend is, no, I wouldn't jump at the chance to have a full head of hair. I've actually reached a point in my life where I've been without hair longer than I was with it and the truth is, I like being smooth of pate. My friends are used to it. I don't frighten small children or make dogs growl. And I don't miss the hair dryers, the shampoos, the tubes and cans of mousse and gel. Or waking up on a pillow that looks like a drop cloth from a service station oil change.

But that's just me. I recognize that some men have their identities wrapped up in what grows out of their skull.

Like the rich, bald Californian who swooped into a barbershop and said to the barber: "I was going to have a hair transplant but I couldn't bear the idea of the pain. Toupees and wigs look silly on me—I WANT REAL HAIR!"

"In fact," he told the barber, "if you can make my hair look like yours without causing me any pain, I'll pay you five thousand dollars!"

So naturally the barber whipped out his razor and shaved his own head.

With a Little Bit of Luck

So this psychiatrist at the University of Hertfordshire decides he wants to study the phenomenon we call "luck." He lines up two groups of volunteers: the first group consists of people who feel they were just "born lucky"; the other group leans toward the philosophy that they'd been short-changed by the Fates and that Life is Unfair.

The shrink gives both groups copies of the same newspaper and asks them to count the photographs. He discovers that the people who consider themselves unlucky take an average of two minutes to count the photos; the "lucky" ones are finished in mere seconds.

Why the spread? The "lucky" folks spotted a notice on the second page that read: "Stop counting. There are forty-three photographs in this paper." The Eyores in the unlucky group were too busy concentrating on counting to spot the notice.

The shrink's conclusion: "Unlucky people miss chance opportunities because they are too focused on looking for something else. They go to a party intent on finding the perfect partner, and so miss an opportunity to make good friends . . . Lucky people are more relaxed and open, and therefore see what is there rather than just what they are looking for."

A roundabout route to the oft-cited observation that we frequently make our own luck.

Frequently, but not always. Consider the case of William Johnson—Blind Willie, to his friends. He was blind because his mother threw lye in his face when he was seven. Life did not noticeably improve for Blind Willie in the years that followed. He grew up impoverished, illiterate and the wrong colour during the Jim Crow years in his home state of Texas. As a young man he was arrested for "inciting a riot." He was only singing a gospel song entitled "If I Had my Way I'd Tear the Building Down"—but he sang it a tad too fervently for the cops' taste. They threw him in jail.

Blind Willie died in 1945 at the age of forty-eight—of hypothermia from sleeping in a sodden bed in the ruins of his house which had burned down two weeks previous.

Not a lot of luck there.

Or consider the life of Eugene Shoemaker, who dreamed of becoming an astronaut and was on his way to achieving it when a routine medical exam revealed he had Addison's disease.

Goodbye astronaut career.

But Shoemaker made his own luck. He took up the study of meteor impact craters on earth and on other planets. He got pretty good at it too—thirty-two comets winging through the heavens now bear his name. One of them, Shoemaker-Levy 9, crashed into Jupiter in 1994. It was the first collision of two solar system bodies ever observed by human beings.

It was also an eerie harbinger of the fate that awaited Shoemaker. Three years later the car he was travelling in crashed and he was killed.

Here comes the lucky part.

His colleagues chose to honour him by placing his ashes aboard a satellite being launched to orbit the moon. It was done, and when the satellite had completed its mission and the battery was about to die, the craft was deliberately crashed into the moon's surface. That's where Shoemaker's ashes will remain for all time, in a titanium capsule inscribed with words from Shakespeare:

> And, when he shall die,
> Take him and cut him out in little stars,
> And he will make the face of heaven so fine
> That all the world will be in love with night,
> And pay no worship to the garish sun.

Blind Willie Johnson didn't end his life on this planet either. His voice is travelling in deep space aboard *Voyager 1*. It's recorded on a gold-plated audio-visual disc that includes the sound of whales, a baby crying, ocean surf—and Blind Willie singing "Dark Was the Night, Cold Was the Ground." It's in a time capsule gift from Earth to whoever, whatever is out there and has the technological capability to appreciate it. The experts don't know how many millennia Willie's song will soar through space, but the ship is bound for the outer limits of our solar system.

Eugene Shoemaker's ashes in an urn on the moon; Blind Willie Johnson's gravelly bass singing the blues for eternity across the cosmos . . .

You and I should get so lucky.

Art—Whatever You Can Get Away With?

Modern Art is what happens when painters stop looking at girls and persuade themselves that they have a better idea.
—John Ciardi

Call me a retrograde male chauvinist Philistine, but I believe Mr. Ciardi had a point. Too bad the American poet kicked the bucket about twenty-five years ago—he could have stuck around and died laughing at the antics of the contemporary British artist Agnieszka Kurant.

Near as I can tell, Ms. Kurant doesn't pay the rent by selling paintings from her studio or through a gallery; she does it by submitting "conceptual pieces" to organizations like Arts Council England. By "conceptual," I mean that Ms. Kurant makes a living selling works of art that do not physically exist. How does that work? Well, recently Ms. Kurant approached Arts Council England with her most recent work.

A blank canvas. Not just a blank canvas, mind—stapled to the canvas was a "notice of intention" from Ms. Kurant indicating that she "plans to paint something on it in the future."

The empty canvas represents a school of artistic philosophy that Ms. Kurant is currently exploring—call it the "less is more, nothing is everything" school. Her sales pitch to the Council also offered a "sculpture" that has not actually been sculpted yet, and a two-hour-and-forty-minute movie she had produced, directed, performed in and filmed.

We'd have to take her word on that too—because she deliberately shot it with no film in her camera.

Lame? You betcha—but it worked. Arts Council England eagerly ponied up the equivalent of $2,300 for the blank canvas, the non-sculpture and the pictureless picture show.

Not only is Ms. Kurant's work lame, it's not even original. The American composer John Cage beat her out by more than half a century with his seminal musical composition called "Four, thirty-three."

It is a three-movement piece composed by Cage back in 1952. He insisted that it was suitable for any instrument or combination of instruments. That means "Four, thirty-three" can be performed on a trumpet or a tuba, a Stradivarius or a banjo, a saxophone or a kazoo. It really doesn't matter if it's performed by a full-dress symphony orchestra in Carnegie Hall or a pickup blues band in a Yonge Street strip joint. Its execution is always exactly, precisely the same: the first movement lasts thirty seconds, the second movement is two minutes, twenty-three seconds, the final movement, one minute and forty seconds.

The result? Cage's masterpiece—"Four, thirty-three," aka 4'33" (do the math). Four minutes and thirty-three seconds.

Of silence.

Or rather, not silence, but random noises—a truck horn, someone coughing, a fly buzzing, the rustle of the musical score as the performer slides through the movements—whatever noise happens while Cage's composition is (not) being played.

For that was Cage's point (as much as he had a point)—that true art should be free from the influence of composer and performer and consist entirely of what the audience experiences.

Which is pretty much the mirror opposite of what most people think of as art. You don't listen to a recording of Pablo Casals to hear traffic noises, go to an art gallery to see blank walls or attend a ballet to stare at an empty stage.

Or am I wrong? Is "art" as we know it—have known it since some Cro Magnon dipped his fingers in red ochre and smeared it on a cave wall—dead? In 2004 Cage's "Four, thirty-three" was voted fortieth place in ABC Radio's Classic 100 all-time great piano pieces. Think about that: four minutes and change of mostly silence speckled with random noise was judged to be superior to works by Beethoven, Bach and Brahms.

Or is it all a shuck—a hustle? "Art," John Cage once said, "is anything you can get away with."

The pop musician Frank Zappa had a more thoughtful take. "The most important thing in art," opined Zappa, "is The Frame. For painting: literally; for other arts: figuratively—because, without this humble appliance, you can't know where The Art stops and The Real World begins. You have to put a 'box' around it because otherwise, what is that shit on the wall?"

Good point, Frank. Good question, too.

Blowing Smoke

I don't smoke. I don't understand what the point is. All I can tell is that these people are addicted to blowing smoke out of their faces. It's not even a good trick.

—BRAD STINE

Brad has a point. The practice of smoking is kind of bedrock goofy when you think of it. There's no cocaine high, no single malt buzz—just an annoying itch that gets momentarily scratched. It's a habit that's smelly, messy, anti-social—and expensive. Cigarettes cost what—ten dollars a pack now? When I was a kid they were twenty-eight cents a pack—thirty-two cents for filter tips. And just about everybody with a spare twenty-eight cents in their pocket indulged: your parents, your teacher, the cop on the beat. Humphrey Bogart smoked and so did Lauren Bacall. Smoking was deeply sexy. Fran Lebowitz, the Gotham wit, famously wrote: "As far as I'm concerned, smoking is the entire point of being an adult." There was a time when that qualified as a droll and witty thing to say. Today . . . not so much.

Is there anyone left who truly thinks smoking is cool? Thanks to anti-smoking legislation, just looking at a package is a turn-off.

When I was a kid cigarette packages didn't come decorated with close-ups of cancerous lungs, ulcerated tongues, rotting teeth or nicotine addicts dragging on a butt through the tracheotomy hole in their throat.

One of the first TV cigarette ads (yes, Virginia, there were such things) featured a showgirl wearing a cigarette package that covered her entire body except for her legs. As she mamboed across the stage an announcer crooned: "No song and dance about medical claims . . . Old Gold cigarettes give you a treat instead of a treatment."

Advertisers were shameless when it came to seducing the audience. Marlboro cigarettes ran a magazine ad that showed a wide-eyed toddler in a diaper gazing adoringly up at his father. The caption read: "Gee Dad, you always get the best of everything—even MARLBORO!" An ad for Viceroy cigarettes showed a stern-looking gent in a white coat. He's saying: "As your dentist, I would recommend Viceroys."

The manufacturers of Camels were the most egregious offenders. There's a magazine ad from 1946 that shows a mother and daughter in consultation with a family GP making a house call (yes, Virginia, we once had those, too). The caption under the photo reads: "113,597 doctors from coast to coast were asked to name the brand they preferred to smoke. Thousands of responses, from general physicians, diagnosticians, surgeons—yes, and nose and throat specialists too—determined that the most named brand was Camel."

Even Santa got into the act. One year around Christmas time the glossy magazines featured full-colour ads of the jolly one tenderly holding a carton of Camels and telling readers: "More smokers prefer Camels than any other cigarette and that holds true for men in the Army, the Navy, the Marines and the Coast Guard too! So remember those lads in uniform . . . remember all the smokers on your list!"

Different times. Innocent times. Most of the major movie stars made extra cash by encouraging the rubes to smoke. Frank Sinatra shilled for Chesterfield; so did Betty Grable, Gary Cooper and Bob Hope. Jean Harlow pushed Lucky Strikes. Lucille Ball flogged Phillip Morris. Movie actress Dolores Del Rio went so far as to try and convince readers that smoking was actually good for them. "I take no chances on an irritated throat," Del Rio says in the ad. "No matter how much I use my voice in acting, I always find Luckies gentle."

There's an old saying among actors: "Sincerity is the most difficult emotion to convey. Once you can fake that, you've got it made." Maybe that's why those early cigarette advertisers raided the Hollywood stables so often. Acting is all about faking sincerity. Take the young fellow who appears in a full-page ad in a 1952 edition of *Life* magazine. He's surrounded by a jumble of cartons of Chesterfield cigarettes. You can tell it must be Christmas season because each cigarette carton has a red ribbon with a gift tag under it. The young fellow is unusually handsome, with coal-black hair and teeth as bright as the white keys on a piano. There's an equally white cigarette stuck between his lips, but it doesn't stop the young fellow from smiling because, as he explains in the caption, "I'm sending Chesterfields to all my friends. That's the merriest Christmas any smoker can have—Chesterfield mildness plus no unpleasant aftertaste."

The young fellow's name is Ronald Reagan.

Smokers . . . Voters . . . If you can fake sincerity, you can sell 'em anything.

Eighty-four and Still Standing

A lot of guys knocked back a couple of Viagra tabs and shuffled down to the newsstand just as fast as their walkers would roll when news got out that they were selling the October issue of *Playboy* magazine for only sixty cents! (They did have to ask the store clerk to help tear off the cellophane wrapper.)

The fire sale price for the monthly mag was a promotional gimmick thought up by the head of the operation—old Priapus himself—Hugh Hefner. Not only has Hef downshifted the price to its original 1960s' level, the October issue itself had a sixties retro vibe to it. The cover featured a—yes!—Playboy bunny with fluffy ears on her head, unlikely boobs spilling out of a too-tight satin bathing suit, a smile as wide as a Steinway keyboard and a tray of cocktails in her hand clearly intended for the Lord of the Manor and guest.

Hef says the whole idea is to celebrate the sixties when Playboy magazine took off and the first Playboy Club was opened.

"It's hard for me to put into words the fact that, obviously, everything changed for me in that time frame," says Hef.

Yep. And then for Hef it never changed again.

For fifty years Hugh Hefner has been living the wet dream of a college frat boy, circa 1960. He rises about noon out of his circular revolving bed, not bothering to change out of his silk pyjamas, greets his covey of Playboy bunnies and assorted Hollywood hangers-on, drinks gallons of Diet Pepsi (up to thirty cans a night) and, well . . . parties on.

Hefner's been living in a cartoon time bubble for half a century, periodically diving into the bunny pool to briefly hook up with a sexual playmate usually answering to a name like Tawny or Candy or Traci (with an "i"). But the names don't really matter. Hef doesn't pay them to hang around and discuss genealogy. They're not so much arm candy as pillow mints.

Playboy Clubs, which back in the heyday twinkled in major cities around the globe, were created to replicate the goings-on in the Playboy mansion in Chicago. Lots of booze, expensive food and, if you didn't squint too hard, waitresses that looked exactly like the signature Playboy magazine playmates—doe-eyed girls with big smiles and amped-up cleavage tricked out as make-believe bunny wabbits, from the perky little rabbit ears on their heads right down to the oversized cotton puff-balls sewed on to their cabooses.

I went into a Playboy Club once, about twenty years ago. I happened to be in New York to tape a radio show, saw the iconic Playboy rabbit head logo on a bronze plaque outside of a club in downtown Manhattan and thought: why not? Inside it was dark and smoky, there was some lounge lizard-y music percolating out of the sound system and a motley collection of male customers scattered singly at tables, most of them wearing cheap, ill-fitting suits. They looked like extras from an off-Broadway production of *Death of a Salesman*.

Talk about losers. These were guys whose idea of a good time was paying to be served drinks by a rabbit with big jugs.

For all Hefner's philosophical gushings about sexual revolution and hip sophistication, these boys looked an awful lot like a gaggle of Johns caught in a back-alley rub 'n tug.

Ah, well, Hefner is nothing if not resilient. Just last year the octogenarian copped some more headlines by announcing his forthcoming wedding to . . . Crystal, I believe it was. Age twenty-four.

The wedding didn't work out (Hef was dumped at the altar) but it provided fodder for more late night one-liners. David Letterman: "Hugh Hefner, eight-four, is marrying his fiancé, aged twenty-four. This guy has Viagra prescriptions older than that."

But who knows? Hefner's nobody's fool and a wily old cuss to boot. Chances are he'll still get the last laugh, much like another octogenarian of note.

After Winston Churchill finished posing for photographs on the occasion of his eightieth birthday the photographer thanked him obsequiously and while packing up his equipment told the British states-man that he "hoped he'd be able to photograph him on his hundredth."

Churchill gazed at the photographer balefully and replied: "I don't see why not, young man. You look reasonably fit to me."

Gather Ye Rosebuds

I've picked up one of the less savoury pastimes that seem to accompany aging: I troll the "obits." Which is to say that each morning I turn with unseemly avidity to the In Memoriam pages of my newspaper to find out who didn't make it through the night.

The Germans, as they often do, have a better word for it—*schadenfreude*: taking delight in the misfortune of others. "Delight" is a touch strong—I don't gloat over the deaths of people but I take some grisly satisfaction when I run across the death notice of some deceased soul whose birth certificate was issued after mine. A curious thing: we spend much of our lives racing to stay ahead of our peers, but the ultimate finish line is one we're all reluctant to cross.

So I check to see who beat me to the finish. More importantly, I check the obits to see if there are any familiar names in there. Last month in the back pages of a college magazine I came across this:

Anthony Etele, formerly of the Ted Rogers School of Business Management, died in January . . .

Could that be Dr. Etele? My grade ten algebra teacher?

The details revealed it could only be Dr. Etele—born in Hungary, 1911—yes, the age would be about right, and he had an accent thicker than a bowl of Magyar goulash. Just reading his name brought his image back to me . . . the ramrod posture, the horseshoe of wispy, well-coiffed hair, the piercing blue eyes.

And the fact that he was not overly fond of having me in his class. Or, for that matter, in his life.

Fair enough. Dr. Etele was a near-genius in the field of numbers and I was an arithmetical klutz. I was shaky on my twelve-times table; when it came to the lofty abstractions of algebra I was hopeless.

So I did what any red-blooded adolescent Canadian school kid would do—I screwed around. I whispered, snickered, threw spitballs and generally disrupted the class. When he had had enough, Dr. Etele would fix those laser blues on me and sonorously intone, "NUH, ARRRRTER BLECK . . . STAND BEFORRRRE DE CLASS! GO FRRRRROM DIS RRRRRROOM AT WANCE!"

And I would pack up my binder and leave with a smirk. I spent a lot of my grade ten algebra classes out in the hall—which helps to explain my mark on the Christmas exam—18 percent.

I didn't dislike Dr. Etele as much as he (justifiably) disliked me. Even in my jerkhood I sensed that there was an indefinable quality about him suggesting that he was much more than a small-time high school math teacher in a hick Ontario town.

Indeed he was. His death notice said that he grew up in Budapest, became a pilot in the 1930s and had a thriving business until the Second World War came along and shot him down. Following the war he fell afoul of the smothering Stalinist death grip that throttled his country, made a Hollywood-movie-worthy escape to Italy and eventually immigrated to Brazil.

What's more he took his first true love, Ilona, with him and started a brand new life in South America. Sometime in the 1950s he and his wife decided to switch continents one more time. They packed up, emigrated again and wound up in Aurora, Ontario, where he landed a job teaching polynomials and linear equations to classrooms full of bored and unimaginative teenage boobs (well, one, anyway).

Our paths never crossed again but I thought of Dr. Etele from time to time in the ensuing decades, mostly with regret. In the arrogance of my youth I'd never cared a damn about the man or his past. I'd have a dozen questions now—where did the "doctor" come from? How many languages did he speak? What was it like to pilot a plane in the 1930s? To escape from Hungary during the Russian occupation? To live in the tropics?

Too late, too late. There's an old poem that goes:

Gather ye rosebuds while ye may,
Old Time is still a-flying

And this same flower that smiles today
Tomorrow will be dying.

Flowers . . . and old math teachers too. The obituary tells me Dr. Etele left behind two sons, seven grandchildren and six great-grandchildren. He was ninety-nine.

There's an ancient Irish anti-war song that contains the refrain "Johnny, we hardly knew ye." When it comes to Dr. Anthony Etele, I didn't know him at all.

My loss.

In Praise of Fat

Here's a heretical notion for you: Fat is Good. That's not just a pudgy columnist thinking wishfully—I've got the Bard to back me up. Shakespeare figured out the upside of corporeal avoirdupois more than four hundred years ago. "Let me have men about me that are fat," he has the doomed Roman leader say near the beginning of *Julius Caesar*. "Yon Cassius has a lean and hungry look; he thinks too much: such men are dangerous."

Good point. Lean Cassius went on to lead the stabbing posse that left Caesar's ventilated corpse sprawled on the steps of the Roman Senate. No surprise really. Most of your major historical bad guys were on the rangy side. Genghis Khan, by all accounts, was cowpoke lanky. Who wouldn't be if they spent their days jouncing in a saddle, a-gallop across the steppes with just short breaks for raping and pillaging? Hitler was skinny; Pol Pot was a beanpole. True, Mussolini was a bit of a porker, but he yearned to be thin—even wore girdles and platform army boots to try and look less rotund.

Contrast those with our earthly pantheon of roly-poly Good Guys: Santa Claus, Buddha, Falstaff, Peter Ustinov, John Candy. Lots of flesh but not a mean bone in the lot.

There was a time when it was meet to have meat on your bones. The "matronly" figure was something to which mature women aspired, while Victorian burghers of business strutted about like pouter pigeons, gold watch chains draped over their ample paunches to emphasize their prosperity. Ironic that in our culture, when food has never been cheaper or more abundant, that the physical ideal is the cadaverous silhouette of a Dickensian workhouse inmate.

Shakespeare continues to be about the last good press chubby folks have received. We know for certain we're not beloved in Biloxi. A couple of years ago Mississippi legislators introduced a bill to make it illegal to serve obese customers in all state-licensed restaurants. The bill wasn't passed but the hostile intent was obvious and the potential implications horrifying. ("Hello, my name is Anthony. Let me just pass this tape measure around your middle to see if I'll be your server tonight.")

Great Britain? Maybe it's a Henry VIII backlash but human heavyweights get even less respect there. Recently the London School of Hygiene and Tropical Medicine issued a report that fingers fatties for everything from rising gas prices to pressure on the world rice markets. The reasoning (I use the term loosely) goes approximately like this: Overweight people eat more than regular people, therefore farmers have to grow more food for them, which has to be processed and distributed, which takes more fuel, which uses more oil, which drives the price of gasoline up while polluting our planet. Plus overweight people drive their cars more than ordinary people because their feet hurt, thus threatening the collapse of civilization as we know it. (I may not have that last part exactly right.)

Hyperbole aside, the imputation is: fat people cause global warming. Can howling mobs with torches and pitchforks be far behind?

My mom could have solved all this nonsense with a flip of her apron. She had a three-letter, one-word mantra for all life's ills—EAT! Lost your job? Love life in the dumps? Can't find your car keys? EAT!

True, it didn't leave her with the profile of a Vogue model—more like a fire hydrant, really—some might even whisper that she was—you know—a Woman of Substance. Fat? Perhaps—but she was fit. Fit enough to chase a twelve-year-old I know down the street with a broom while she was six months pregnant.

Would have caught me too if I hadn't been on my bike.

Sir John Mortimer said it best: "I refuse to spend my life worrying about what I eat," the British author harrumphed. "There's no pleasure worth forgoing for an extra three years in the geriatric ward."

I wish I'd had the opportunity to break bread with Sir John; he sounds downright jolly. I know he'd have been welcome at Mom's dinner table anytime.

Tombstone Tales

I've got my first stop picked out for my next visit to Paris and it's not the Louvre, the Eiffel Tower or a café on the Left Bank. It's a leafy, 109-acre sanctuary in the twentieth *arrondissement*—Père Lachaise, the most famous cemetery in the world.

Darned near everybody who was anybody is in there—and not just those of the Gallic persuasion. Oscar Wilde is buried in Père Lachaise, along with Proust, Balzac and Colette. Gertrude Stein, unlike her pronouncement on Oakland, California, is there; so is Isadora Duncan. Artists? Delacroix, Doré, Pissarro, Seurat. Composers? Chopin, Enescu. Entertainers? Yves Montand, Edith Piaf, Sarah Bernhardt, Maria Callas. There's even plot space for a hell-raiser like Jim Morrison of the Doors.

Père Lachaise is probably the ultimate trip for cemetery cruisers but truth to tell I don't need to visit a celebrity graveyard to enjoy my darker side. Pretty well any marble orchard will do. I love the cemetery ambiance although I don't usually admit it out loud—not after I blurted it out at a cocktail party one evening. "What are your hobbies?" a woman asked. "Walking," I said. "Me too," she said. "Where do you hike?"

"Cemeteries mostly," I said. She looked at me woodenly and muttered: "You're creeping me out."

Her loss. Cemeteries are splendid places to perambulate at leisure. Generously treed and lovingly landscaped, devoid of vehicular traffic and commercial eye clutter—and of course, pleasingly silent.

Why not? Everybody's sleeping.

And unless there's a funeral in progress most cemeteries are deserted. I can't for the life of me understand why. I've walked in unfamiliar cemeteries for decades and never once been asked to leave. As long as you don't bring a picnic and a boom box the authorities won't bother you. And it's not as if the residents are going to complain.

No need to bring along a paperback or a newspaper, there's plenty of reading material in the cemetery, much of it poignant. The information is Hemingway-esque—simple, but freighted with meaning. A cracked marble stone tells you that the woman beneath it was born in 1899, died 1918, along with her infant Melissa. Hmmm . . . the Spanish flu pandemic? Or did she die in childbirth? Only nineteen years old. Was her husband overseas? Missing in action? You can almost feel a short story writing itself.

And then there are the epitaphs. Most of them are generic and clichéd: At Rest; Gone But Not Forgotten; Asleep in the Arms of Jesus; Ready to Meet My Maker. Those are the boring ones. They sound uninspired, mechanical; the mortician's equivalent of the Hallmark card.

But some folks, bless 'em, realize that the blank space on their tombstone represents their last best chance to sum up in a few chiselled words, what their whole life has meant to them. An epitaph is the ultimate in afterthoughts.

Some are gloomy—the stone over poet Charles Bukowski's grave reads: I NEVER LIKED IT ANYHOW. W.C. Fields gravestone is popularly believed to say ON THE WHOLE, I'D RATHER BE IN PHILADELPHIA. A flint-hearted, defiantly anonymous Vermonter saw to it that his tombstone read: I WAS SOMEBODY. WHO, IS NO BUSINESS OF YOURS.

Other epitaph writers choose to leave us with a smile on our faces. Johnny Carson's choice? I'LL BE RIGHT BACK. Phyllis Diller wants her epitaph to read I DIED LAUGHING. Larry King has opted for HE FINALLY MET A DEADLINE.

Canada's own W.P. Kinsella has his afterlife all planned out. He intends to spend it under a stone with the inscription: AT LAST, TIME TO CATCH UP ON MY READING.

There is reported to be in (where else?) the Boot Hill Cemetery in (where else?) Tombstone, Arizona, a headstone over the grave of one Lester Moore, an ex-Wells Fargo cargo agent that reads:

HERE LIES LESTER MOORE
FOUR SLUGS FROM A .44
NO LESS, NO MORE.

Leave 'em laughing—good advice for comedians and cadavers alike. I reckon the only big mistake an epitaph writer can make is to take him or herself too seriously. The robustly egoed author Vladimir Nabokov penned his own epitaph in his book *Pale Fire*. "Other men die," wrote Nabokov, "but I am not another; therefore I'll not die."

But that's not the tale a tombstone in the Cimitière de Clarens in Montreux, Switzerland, tells. It reads: VLADIMIR NABOKOV 1899–1977.

Top of the World, Ma!

Dear Mother, I am alright. Stop worrying about me.
———Letter from a seventeen-year-old Egyptian girl

She never will, of course. That's what moms do, be they from Egypt, Ethiopia or Eglinton Avenue West. They do worry and they do hang on. It's their job.

Uncharitable observers sometimes put it down to a power grab on mom's part—and there has been a bit of that down through history. Legend has it that a soothsayer once told Agrippina, heavy with child, that her offspring if he lived would become Emperor of Rome—also that he would murder his mother. Agrippina, keeping her eye on the job security ball, replied. "Let him kill me, then."

Her child—a psychopathic little monster named Nero—eventually achieved both goals.

Two millennia later and many miles north and west another mother nurtured an infant amid dreams of monarchical glory. The Duchess of Kent groomed her little princess for the British throne virtually from birth. The princess lived with mommy dearest twenty-four cloistered hours a day. The child was forbidden to speak to anyone except in the presence of mother or her strict German governess. On the day of her ascension to the throne the Duchess of Kent asked her newly crowned daughter, barely eighteen, if there was anything else mommy could do for her. "I wish to be left alone," she replied. The new queen's wish was everyone's command. Her bed was removed from her mother's chambers that very day and young Victoria began her sixty-five-year reign over the British Empire.

With, I have no doubt, her mother clucking and tut-tutting impotently in the wings.

It's just what mothers do. A playwright by the name of Florida Scott-Maxwell observed: "No matter how old a mother is, she watches her middle-aged children for signs of improvement." I endorse the notion. My mom, bless her, slackened the apron strings enough to let me go to sea at sixteen and to Europe with a backpack at twenty. A few years later when it became clear that I would scribble for a living, she gave that her blessing too. But not wholeheartedly. I remember telling her that I had a cushy new job with my own office—a secretary, even—in the PR department of a prestigious international company. She smiled encouragingly, patted my hand and turned away, murmuring something.

"What'd she say?" I asked my older, brighter sister. My sister shook her head—sibling code for "Not now, stupid. I'll tell you later."

When Mom went out to the kitchen my sister leaned over and said, "She's very happy about your success—she just wishes you had a real trade to fall back on."

My mom was a farm girl. She came from Real Life where people worked up a sweat and strained their backs and soaked their aching feet in a basin full of hot water and Epsom salts at the end of the day. I don't think she ever quite believed that the world contained people dumb enough to pay her son for rearranging words on a page.

It wasn't that she was disappointed in me, just apprehensive . . . that someday reality might give me a cuff on the back of the head.

Good old Mom. If she was still around I'd make her smile with my best Jimmy Cagney impression. "Top of the world, Ma!" I'd cry, waving my arms like Sid Crosby in overtime.

And she would remind me that in the movie Cagney got tear-gassed, plugged full of bullet holes and blown up along with the gasoline storage tank he was standing on.

Moms worry. They can't help it.

T'was ever thus. That note from the Egyptian girl I mentioned at the top? You'll find it in the Metropolitan Museum of Art. It was written on papyrus. About four thousand years ago.

While My Guitar Gently Sleeps

I am a senior citizen, which means I have achieved Official Old Fart status. And now that I've reached the age of certified decrepitude I need to make a confession.

This was not the life I intended to lead.

I had expected by now to be unspeakably rich, bedevilled by paparazzi and pursued by ecstatic, clamouring groupies wherever I went.

My plan was to become an International Guitar Legend.

My musical North Star was the great and tragic Lenny Breau, the most talented guitarist Canada (perhaps the world) ever had. But I also worshipped at the altars of Robert Johnson, Chet Atkins, Jimi Hendrix, Les Paul, Ellen McIlwaine, Santana and Gordy Farmer, the kid across the street who showed me how to nail down a three-finger G-chord.

I immersed myself in Guitar Legend territory whenever and wherever I could. I hung around dank and draughty coffee houses drinking chipped mugs of vile, over-priced java and listening to the local, I use the word loosely, talent. I bought tickets for Cockburn and Lightfoot and Joni Mitchell when they passed through. I haunted the guitar section of the local music store and spent my school lunch money on glossy instruction manuals for Jazz Guitar, Folk Guitar, Blues Guitar, Bluegrass Guitar and of course, Basic Guitar for Dummies. I grew warty-looking calluses on my fingertips and wilfully deformed the muscles in my left forearm until I was strong enough to form barre chords.

I was in love with the guitar. Not just the sounds it could make but the hippy, sinuous, sensuous look and feel and scent of it. I got as close to guitars as I could and dreamed of getting closer. If B.B. King had stopped for gas in my town I'd have washed his limo for free. With my tongue. I fantasized of hitchhiking to Graceland humping a backpack full of jars of Ma Weston's crunchy peanut butter and a side of Canada Packers back bacon, the better to endear myself to Elvis. Even today I live within a Rolling Stone's throw of three of Canada's greatest Guitar Legends—Valdy, Bill Henderson and Randy Bachman. Coincidence? I think not. More like kismet.

Yep, me and guitars, we go back a ways. Got my first six-string in the pre-Woodstock era, when Neil Young was a pup and little Bobby Zimmerman was down at the Hibbing, Minnesota, Greyhound depot trying to decipher the bus departures for New York City. Since then I've owned a succession of six-strings, twelve-strings—even a little Martin Backpack guitar. It's about the size of a ukulele—just right for taking on road trips and camping weekends.

So it follows, does it not, that like Johnny B. Goode, I can "play that guitar just like a-ringin' a bell"? Got my Django Reinhardt chops down cold? Able to reel off "Classical Gas" and "Stairway to Heaven" in my sleep?

It does not.

I shudder to think how many hours I have spent over the past (God!) forty years hunched over a guitar trying to coax something musical out of its sullen little sound hole. I wince when I think of the money I've lashed out—not just for my guitars but for guitar lessons, guitar strings, capos and flat, finger and thumb picks.

Because here's the thing: Do you know what I can play on a guitar after thousands of dollars and forty years and God knows how many hours of plucking and strumming and fretting and bleeding—do you know what I can play?

"Freight Train."

As in:

> Freight train, freight train goin' so fast
> Freight train, freight train goin' so fast
> Please don't tell what train I'm on
> So they won't know where I've gone.

That's it! Four brain-dead simple chords—C, G7, E7, F—a simple blues ditty that a chimpanzee wearing boxing gloves could figure out and play in fifteen minutes.

And when I play it, it still sounds like Dr. Bundolo's Amateur Hour.

The simple truth that I could never grasp was that I was in love with the idea of being a guitar player—despite abundant evidence that I had ten left thumbs and no talent for the instrument whatsoever.

Ah well, I wasn't alone. Just think of all the unplayed guitars mouldering away in cupboards and attics and storerooms across the land.

I finally packed mine up and gave them away so that I wouldn't have to feel guilty looking at them anymore.

It took a few decades and a touch of arthritis in my fingerpicking hand but I think I've finally accepted it: I get an F in Guitar Theory and Practice.

But an A-plus in Pigheadedness.

Tit for Tat

When I was sixteen I went to sea for the summer with a crew of Jamaicans on an oil tanker that ran between Halifax and Venezuela. I came back in the fall to start grade twelve with thirty-six dollars, a rather impressive repertoire of Spanish and Jamaican expletives . . .

And a tattoo.

Nothing flamboyant—a simple anchor with a banner entwined around it, all discreetly drilled into my upper right arm. Such a piddly tattoo wouldn't have raised an eyebrow in Halifax, St. John's or Vancouver but I lived in rural southern Ontario. Deepest Landlubberville. There was no tradition in those parts of going to sea and certainly no history of inking one's carcass. I stood out. My English teacher took one look at my shiny tattoo and sniffed, "Two types of people get tattoos: pirates and jailbirds."

Music to my ears. I was suddenly an NGOC—Notorious Guy on Campus.

Times change. To achieve notoriety on campus nowadays you'd have to be the only student without a tattoo. Nowadays girls have them. Geeks and nerds have them. Hell, the teachers have them.

No surprise. Humankind has been fascinated with tattoos for ages. Ancient Egyptians fooled around with tattoos as did most every culture from the High Arctic to Polynesia. In 1991 scientists chipped the frozen corpse of a Late Stone Age hunter out of an alpine glacier and guess what they found on his body? Fifty-seven tattoos—on his back, behind one knee and around both ankles. The hunter died about 5,300 years ago.

The tattoos weren't fancy, just squiggles and dots really. Not like the ones you see today. Modern tattoos are expansive, intricate and more colourful than a Toller Cranston canvas.

Complicated, too. There's a woman in Toronto who has Jack Kerouac all over her back. The closing lines from Kerouac's novel *On the Road* run across her dorsal surface from left collarbone to lower right ribcage. And just in case some random reader isn't familiar with the work there's an image of Kerouac hunched over a typewriter superimposed over the script.

It's pretty impressive but if I may be so bold . . . what's the point? I get the erotic potential of a butterfly on the buttock or a pixie dancing up a thigh—but half a novel on your back? You'd have to join a nudist camp to be appreciated.

Even then you'd always be standing still for slow readers.

There's some evidence that the tattoo cult has jumped the shark. The actress Susan Sarandon has the names of her kids tattooed down her spine (is she worried she'll forget?). When Lindsay Lohan gets bored (which is often, apparently) she can always look down at her right wrist and read her mantra: STARS: ALL WE ASK FOR IS OUR RIGHT TO TWINKLE.

And then there's the actress Megan Fox, who is rapidly transforming herself into a walking bookmobile. One of her more recent tattoos is a disjointed line of text that rambles across her belly from right hip to left breast. It reads: "Those who danced were thought to be quite insane by those who could not hear the music."

"It's a quote from Nietzsche," Fox explained to a TV interviewer airily.

Except it isn't. Nietzsche never said it. It's an urban legend. Like Sarah Palin's grasp of geography.

That's the thing about tattoos. If you're going to get one with words in it, make sure your designated mutilator consults a dictionary.

Unlike the woman who had a ruby red heart tattooed on her chest and below it the caption in large flowing cursive: BEAUTIFUL TRADGEDY.

Or the guy who paid a lot of dough to have his personal motto needled into his back in huge gothic letters.

It reads: I'M AWSOME.

Even tattoos without words in them can prove embarrassing. Never forget the one law that none of us can break—the law of gravity.

That beautiful young thing with the cute, perky little hummingbird tattoo peeking out of her cleavage?

Give her a few Big Macs, a desk job and a couple of decades, it'll stretch into a pterodactyl.

Lies I Told My Father

I don't remember the first lie I ever told but I recall my first real whopper. We were father-bragging, Johnnie Carlton and I—aged seven or thereabouts. Johnnie had just assured me that his pop could easily whup my pop in a fist fight. Gravely I nodded toward Johnnie's house nearby.

"My father," I muttered in menacing falsetto, "could lift your house."

It wasn't a flagrant falsehood because part of me really believed the words as they came out of my mouth. I could visualize my old man hitching his pants, spitting on his hands, doing a deep knee bend, grabbing the foundation and actually hoisting the Carlton bungalow out of the dirt.

Boys will be boys. Johnnie Carlton's dad was a paunchy academic with doughy, schoolteacher hands embedded with blackboard chalk dust; my dad was a heavy-smoking, bald-headed cattle salesman with a touch of diabetes and an incipient heart condition. Neither of them, I venture to guess, would ever be on Don Cherry's speed dial.

Mortals both, but to the two of us they were giants. Even though my dad topped out at about five foot seven.

Lesson number one: Volume doesn't equal worth. As the old bluesman Jimmy Reed sang in "Big Boss Man": "You ain't big. You tall, that's all."

A kid learns a lot just by hanging out with his dad, sussing out the rhythms and the idiosyncrasies of manhood. The lessons aren't always positive. I remember being in the old Eaton's department store in

Toronto with my dad, looking for the toy department. I scooted away, found a salesman and asked directions. "It's on the fourth floor," I reported proudly to my father, certain he'd be impressed by my Cub Scout initiative.

Instead he wore a look of slight exasperation. "I know where the toy department is," he said quietly. "You didn't have to ask."

Lesson number two: Real Men don't ask directions. They just puff up and pretend they know where they're going.

You win some, you lose some. Fatherhood only offers on-the-job training and there's no reliable instruction manual. There is the old story about the brand new father taking his wife and baby home from the hospital for the first time. "Any questions?" asks the pediatrician.

"Just one, doctor," says the dad. "What time should we wake the little guy in the morning?"

In our house we kept the house keys in a glass bowl on a sideboard in the front hall. One day, fooling around, I knocked the bowl off and it shattered on the floor. How to handle it? Pass the buck. That evening my dad called me over to his chair where he was reading the paper. "What happened to the glass bowl?" he asked.

"Jimmy broke it," I lied.

My father gave me an appraising look, rolled up the front section of the *Toronto Star* and said in a calm voice, "Your brother is four years old. He couldn't reach that high. I believe you broke the bowl and I believe you're going to lose two weeks' allowance to pay for it."

I was red-faced, tongue-tied and guilty as hell. He wasn't quite finished. He took the rolled-up newspaper, tapped me on the forehead and added: "And that's for lying."

The newspaper tap was powder-puff light and wouldn't have bruised a gnat. He might as well have slugged me with a tire iron. I'd never felt so devastated. I won't say I never lied again but friends assure me I never lie convincingly.

My pop blew it on asking directions but when it came to the consequences of not telling the truth he knocked it out of the park. That's the way it goes between fathers and their kids. There's another story about old Joe Kennedy, the American patriarch, dandling his granddaughter Caroline on his knee, marvelling at her precociousness.

"She's very bright, Jack," said Joe to the girl's father. "Much brighter than you were at her age."

"Yes, she is," responded JFK. "But look who she has for a father."

Suitably Dressed—Not

Passed a businessman waiting at a bus stop this morning. He was dressed to the nines in what looked like a posh Harry Rosen three-piece. The suit looked great; the guy wearing it—not so much. He had his arms crossed and his hands stuffed in his armpits, his shoulders shrugged up around his ears and he was stamping his Gucci loafers up and down like a flamenco dancer with a stutter. Very stylish—aside from the fact that he was in Canada and he was freezing to death. The things we do for fashion.

Well . . . not all of us. I worked for the Canadian Broadcasting Corporation for thirty years and do you know what the very best thing about the job was? No dress code.

Actually there was an informal dress code but it was defined by what you didn't, rather than what you did, wear. We could show up for duty wearing Levi's, Bermuda shorts, football sweaters, stretch pants, Hawaiian shirts, tie-dyed T-shirts—we could come to work wearing pith helmets and frogman flippers if we felt like it.

What a guy didn't wear was a suit. If you came to work in a business suit it meant you were getting married, on your way to a funeral or even worse, you were One of Them: a CBC executive. A paper-pushing, bureaucratic lifer. Aka a dork.

We had an epithet for such people. We called them "Suits."

Those who pooh-poohed the CBC (including the Conservatives, Don Cherry and most of Alberta) considered our Bohemian attire just one more sign of the corporation's Bolshevik, anarchist leanings but I believe we were actually ahead of our time, because if there is one word that sums up the typical business suit as worn by the Canadian male, that word would be "stupid."

It makes no sense, people! We live in a climate that is six months sub-polar and six months semi-tropical. The business suit is both too flimsy to protect us from Arctic chill and too hot to bear when the summer sun beats down.

And the necktie? Don't get me started on neckties.

Do you know why eleven gazillion businessmen around the world voluntarily half-garrotte themselves every working morning by cinching a coloured ribbon around their necks? It's because about two centuries ago a troop of Croatian cavalrymen galloped into Versailles for a visit. They all wore colourful neckerchiefs and some demoiselle close to Louis XIV fluttered her fan and murmured, "C'est beau!" Lou agreed. The fashion of the "Croat," or as it became corrupted, "cravat," was born.

When you look at it the entire business suit is a hoary hangover from our long-vanished military past. Padded shoulders? A nod to the epaulettes that still decorate most military uniforms. Those odd and utterly useless lapels? A modification of old-time military greatcoats. The buttons on the suit sleeves perform no function other than to hearken back to the days when officers displayed their rank by brass "pips."

Ever wondered why men's suit jackets have vents up the back? That's so we'll be more comfortable in the saddle as we ride our warhorses in a victory charge.

The wacky fact is, this bizarre, mongrelized outfit is the accepted workday uniform of millions of businessmen from Tokyo to Toronto and from Prince Rupert to Port au Prince. And it doesn't much matter what the wearer does for a living. Bankers wear suits; so do gangsters. Prime ministers, pimps, trade union leaders, riverboat gamblers—they all "suit up" each morning in a jacket and trousers, shirt and tie.

As they have—with minor variations in lapel width and button placement—for the past 150 years.

The business suit is the fashion equivalent of the cockroach: it survives—somehow—in climates that range from Arctic winter to equatorial summer. And I might as well confess that even though I no longer punch a clock I still own a business suit. It's a dark blue number that resides in a drycleaner's plastic bag at the back of my cupboard. It hangs in semi-permanent hibernation, only emerging for weddings and funerals. I hardly ever have to put it on or even see it but it still annoys me, hanging there, like a large, morbid bat behind my brighter, more sensible apparel. I'd feel more comfortable with it if it featured some realistic attachments. Like, say, a snap-on parka hood and a detachable lining that could double as a beach towel.

Now THAT would be a Canadian business suit.

Too Smart for His Own Good

Who do you reckon is the smartest man who ever lived?

King Solomon has a pretty good rep in the wisdom department. Signor da Vinci was a veritable mental giant and Shakespeare was certainly no dummy. The nineteenth-century British philosopher John Stuart Mill was quick off the blocks—by the age of ten he was reading Plato and Demosthenes in the original Greek. Closer to our own time, Mr. Einstein was undeniably impressive.

But all things considered I think I'd have to give the nod to Mr. William James Sidis.

The movie *Good Will Hunting* was loosely based on his life, but Hollywood, *comme toujours*, goosed the truth and rouged the details until the cinematic product bore little resemblance to the flesh and blood original. There was no need for that. The real life of William James Sidis was sufficiently remarkable to stand alone.

Sidis was born in Boston, Massachusetts, in 1898 and it wasn't long before the Sidis household realized they had a child prodigy on their hands. He learned to spell in English at the age of one, moved on to French and German by the age of four. By the time other children were starting kindergarten the child was speaking and reading Russian, Hebrew, Turkish and Armenian as well.

He wasn't merely a language whiz, he excelled at maths, too. Care to know what day of the week Caesar was assassinated or the Siege of Troy began? Little Billy Sidis could tell you. He could name the day of the week on which any historical event occurred thanks to a complicated system he came up with. At the age of five.

Three years later at, yes, the age of eight, Sidis applied for entrance to the Massachusetts Institute of Technology. He scored an unheard-of 100 percent on the entrance exam. He entered Harvard at the age of eleven and graduated with first-class honours before he was old enough to legally drive a car. By twenty he was a mathematics professor at Texas Rice Institute where he taught Euclidian geometry, non-Euclidean geometry and trigonometry.

Oh, yeah . . . he was drop-dead good-looking too.

But there was a dark side to Sidis' blazing accomplishments. Putting a brain like his in a normal human body was like welding a Ferrari engine onto a roller skate. Sidis had his first nervous breakdown at twelve. He recovered—sort of—but he was walking a fine line from then on. The professorship didn't work out. "I'm not much of a teacher," Sidis confessed. "I didn't leave—I was asked to go." The same year he got fired Sidis was arrested for participating in a violent demonstration and sentenced to eighteen months in jail. Influential friends kept him out of prison and he was shipped off to a sanatorium.

For the rest of his short life (he died of a cerebral haemorrhage at the age of forty-six) William Sidis lived pretty much in obscurity. He held only menial jobs and became a self-proclaimed peridromophile—someone with a fascination for streetcar transportation. Indeed, Sidis collected streetcar transfers as a hobby.

Newspapers and magazines love these "How the Mighty Are Fallen" stories. In 1937 the *New Yorker* magazine published a long piece on him under the title "Where Are They Now?" It described the one-time child genius as a lonely and largely forgotten down-and-outer eking out his days in a tiny "hall bedroom in Boston's shabby South End."

Down, maybe—but not out. Sidis sued the magazine for defamation and won.

In fact the Sidis story isn't a simple riches-to-rags morality tale. He spent the last half of his life in anonymity but he was far from enfeebled. He was a writing machine. Under pseudonyms like Frank Folupa, Barry Mulligan and William Edward Beals Jr., Sidis wrote treatises on everything from cosmology to American Indian history, from anthropology to transport system theory. He invented a language (Vendergood) and a grammar to go with it. He predicted the existence of black holes in space decades before astrophysicists confirmed it.

Was he a genius? And then some. He had an intellect that ranged wider than Leonardo da Vinci's. Most of us are lucky to have an IQ north of 100. Experts estimate Albert Einstein's was 168.

William Sidis was somewhere between 250 and 300.

And yet he wound up, if not a failure, certainly not bathed in glory and adulation. An intellectual named Richard Hofstadter once said: "No one who lives among intellectuals is likely to idealize them unduly."

I think the humorist Josh Billings said it best: "Some folks are wise," said Billings, "some otherwise."

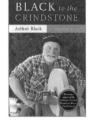
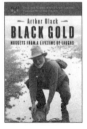